P9-CKF-623

Published by PERIPLUS EDITIONS (HK) LTD.,
with editorial offices at
153 Milk Street
Boston MA 02109 and
5 Little Road #08-01
Singapore 536983.

Library of Congress Cataloging-in-Publication Data

DeWitt, Dave.
The food of Santa Fe : authentic recipes from the American Southwest / recipes by Nancy Gerlach ; text by Dave DeWitt ; food photography by Eduardo Fuss.
p. cm.
Includes index.
ISBN 9625932291. — ISBN 9625931023 (PLC)
1. Cookery—New Mexico—Santa Fe. 2. Cookery, American—Southwestern style. 3. Santa Fe (N.M.)—Social life and customs. I. Gerlach, Nancy.
TX715.D4952 1998
641.5979—dc21 947-32182
CIP

Photo Credits:
The photo on page 17 is by T. Harmon Parkhurst (neg. # 68822) and is reproduced courtesy of the Photo Archives at the Palace of Governors, Santa Fe. The painting on the endpapers is by Amanda Grogan.

Distributed by

USA
Charles E. Tuttle Co., Inc.
RR 1 Box 231-5
North Clarendon, VT 05759-9700
Tel.: (802) 773-8930
Fax.: (802) 773-6993

Japan
Tuttle Shokai Ltd.
1-21-13, Seki, Tama-ku,
Kawasaki-shi
Kanagawa-ken 214, Japan
Tel.: (044) 833-0225
Fax.: (044) 822-0413

Asia-Pacific
Berkeley Books Pte. Ltd.
5 Little Road #08-01
Singapore 536983
Tel.: (65) 280-3320
Fax.: (65) 280-6290

First edition

1 3 5 7 9 10 8 6 4 2
06 05 04 03 02 01 00 99 98

PRINTED IN THE REPUBLIC OF SINGAPORE

THE FOOD OF SANTA FE

Authentic Recipes from the American Southwest

Essays and recipes by Dave DeWitt and Nancy Gerlach
Photography by Eduardo Fuss
Styling by Christina Ong

Additional recipes from:
Kit Baum, El Farol
Jeff Copeland, Santacafé
Paul Hunsicker, Paul's Restaurant of Santa Fe
Katharine Kagel, Cafe Pasqual's
Mark Kiffin and Andrew MacLauchlan, Coyote Cafe
Al Lucero, Maria's New Mexican Kitchen
Rosalea Murphy, The Pink Adobe
Flynt Payne, Inn of the Anasazi
Kelly Rogers, La Casa Sena
Santa Fe School of Cooking
Maurice Zeck, La Fonda

PERIPLUS

PERIPLUS
EDITIONS

Contents

PART ONE: FOOD IN SANTA FE

PART TWO: COOKING IN SANTA FE

PART THREE: THE RECIPES

APPENDIX

Part One: Food in Santa Fe

The City Different melds local traditions with a hip, modern style

In just a few short decades, Santa Fe has become the magical city of the Southwest, a destination for artists, writers, chefs, and, of course, tourists. Nicknamed The City Different, Santa Fe's reputation for tolerating individuality has had much to do with its attraction as a place to live. Its tremendous appeal as a trendy place to visit is the result of countless articles and books about the landscape, the art scene, the cuisine, the architecture and the Santa Fe look in clothing and jewelry—all part of what is termed Santa Fe style. And though its overexposure has fostered a certain Santa Fe blasé, there is just no denying the incredible charm of the place.

The city is on a high desert mesa at seven thousand feet above sea level, offering spectacular views of the Sangre de Cristo Mountains that tower above it. The sun always seems to shine in Santa Fe and the quality of the light and the beauty of the mesas have drawn artists to the city for decades. The city's adobe architecture, unchanged for centuries, reveals Santa Fe's deep Native American roots. The buildings in the historic district—even new ones—all share the same ocher color and smooth mud finish.

Santa Fe residents view the huge influx of tourists each year as just a continuation of history. After all, during the past four hundred years Sante Fe has been controlled by Native Americans, Spaniards, Mexicans, Americans and Confederates. Each of these groups helped create the flavors of Santa Fe.

The first food fusion of Santa Fe occurred when Spanish settlers from Mexico founded the city in 1598, bringing European and Mexican ingredients that were combined with the corn cuisine of the native Pueblo Indians. New Mexican cuisine can thus be viewed as the northernmost of the Mexican regional cuisines; it is also the spiciest because of the New Mexicans' love of chile peppers. The second food fusion occurred when Anglo-Americans arrived with new ingredients, recipes and restaurants offering the standard meat and potatoes of the eastern United States. But what has really placed Santa Fe on the culinary map has occurred during the last twenty-five years: a proliferation of fine restaurants that have vastly expanded the concept of Southwestern cooking.

Many of Santa Fe's restaurants are the epitome of the concept of fusion, offering dishes that bridge the culinary gaps between cultures. Despite the international flavors, traditions are still strong. In homes and restaurants the visitor will still discover the delicious New Mexican dishes that depend upon the most basic New World ingredients: corn, beans, squash, and chile peppers.

Page 2: *Its spectacular buildings, which echo the color and form of the surrounding hills, make Taos Pueblo one of the most famous pueblos in New Mexico.*
Opposite: *A hand-crafted* santo, *or saint, sits watch over a festive Christmas meal of* posole *(left) and* chicos *(recipes on pages 130–31).*

Native Americans and Their Food

An ancient culinary heritage of wild game and native plants

When the first Spanish explorers ventured north from Mexico City in the sixteenth century and wandered into what is now the American Southwest, they encountered the descendants of a great prehistoric civilization, the Anasazi. These Native Americans, known as the Pueblo Indians, were clustered along the Rio Grande near present-day Santa Fe in separate villages, or pueblos. They made excellent use of nearly every edible animal and plant substance imaginable. For protein, the Native Americans hunted and trapped deer, rabbits, quail, pronghorn, bison, and many other mammals and birds. The meat of this game was usually grilled over coals or added to a pot and turned into a stew.

Corn is held sacred by Native Americans and has been an important part of the Southwestern diet for centuries. The rich colors of this Indian corn only appear once the corn has dried; when it is fresh the corn is a more subdued yellow or white.

However, some tribes (such as the Apaches) had taboos against eating certain animals that they regarded as repulsive: snakes, fish and owls, for example. Later on, after the appearance of European food animals, game was viewed as "poor man's meat." Today, of course, game has made a comeback because of its exotic nature and appeal to adventurous diners.

The food plants eaten by the Native Americans were divided into two categories: those harvested in the wild and those cultivated plants that had managed to adapt to the dry desert climate or were irrigated. Harvested wild plants included acorns (from which flour was made), berries such as chokecherry and juniper, yucca fruits, various herbs such as wild mint, mushrooms, mesquite seeds (sometimes called beans) and agave hearts (*mescal*), which were roasted in pits by the Mescalero Apaches and other tribes. Three other uncultivated crops were very important in Native American cooking (and are most commonly used today): cacti, piñon nuts, and *chiltepíns* (wild, berrylike chile peppers). The cactus fruits and leaves were usually eaten raw, as in salads, while the piñon nuts were usually mixed with honey as a snack or dessert. *Chiltepíns* were used as a pungent spice before the Spanish introduced domesticated chiles.

Even though wild crops were important, the ancient Anasazi culture of the Southwest—and later the Pueblo Indians—depended on some important domesticated crops: corn, beans, squash, and (after the Spanish arrived) chile peppers. It is not a coincidence that these foods are the foundation of Southwestern cuisine. Although domesticated in Mexico and Central America, these crops had moved north to what is now New Mexico long before the Spanish arrived.

The Anasazis, ancestors of the the builders of the Taos Pueblo, built these cliff dwellings at Mesa Verde in Colorado. At one time close to five thousand people lived on Mesa Verde in two- and three-hundred-room apartment houses.

Here in New Mexico we not only claim the oldest regional cuisine in the United States but continue to enjoy many of the foods that have been part of the Native American diet for hundreds or even thousands of years. Despite the influences of these ingredients, Native American cuisine these days has mostly been incorporated into what has become New Mexican cuisine, so wild plants and game are no longer as common as they once were.

Corn is so important to Native Americans that it serves as the basis of the cuisine and also plays a pivotal role in their religion and many of their ceremonies. The four kinds of corn—yellow, white, red and blue—were a gift from the gods or creator who taught the people how to plant, harvest, and use it before they were allowed to walk Mother Earth.

Beans, domesticated ten thousand years ago in Peru, even predate cultivated corn. Easy to grow and store, beans quickly became an essential part of the Native American diet. The Hopi grow fourteen kinds of beans in a variety of colors, which when combined with corn provide a complete protein source for times when game is scarce.

Chile, another staple in the diet, was domesticated in both South and Central America about the same time as beans and also migrated north. And although there is little doubt that domesticated chile was introduced to Native Americans of the Southwest by the Spaniards, there is evidence that at least the wild *chiltepín* was already growing in the Southwest when the Spaniards arrived.

One way to get a feel of the life of Native Americans and a taste of their version of New Mexican cuisine is to visit a pueblo. In the fall, with chile sun-drying on roofs or hung in strings (*ristras*) and corn stacked around the pueblo to dry, it is almost like stepping back in time. Occasionally, visitors are invited into homes for some food. Many of the dishes, such as enchiladas and tamales, show a Hispanic influence, but there are a few specialties that are uniquely Indian. Interestingly enough, most Indian dishes today are made with ingredients imported by Europeans rather than with native foods that still exist in abundance.

***Right:** Pueblo religious ceremonies were usually held in underground rooms—usually round—called* kivas. *This wall painting is in a kiva at the Coronado State Monument, fifty miles southwest of Santa Fe.*
***Opposite:** The Deer Dance at San Juan Pueblo, which takes place in February, is performed by the young people of the tribe to honor the deer for the many gifts he has given them. The profile of a deer dancer is the symbol of the San Juan Pueblo people.*

Mutton stew was probably imported into the pueblos in the Santa Fe area from the Navajos, who live farther west. The Navajos were sheepherders whose sheep were originally from Mexico by way of Spain. The origin of fry bread, the bread that puffs up when it is fried in oil (lard is preferred) seems to be Navajo as well. Interestingly, a smaller version of this bread, called *sopaipillas,* is served in Santa Fe and Albuquerque restaurants. Wheat was imported by the Europeans; few Indians today cook with acorn flour. One traditional bread that probably antedates the Europeans is blue corn bread; undoubtedly, there was an earlier form of it that lacked the baking powder and milk used today. It is made with flour from Indian blue corn, and its brilliant blue color can be disconcerting to those not accustomed to it.

Other dishes likely to be encountered at the pueblos are fried red chiles, dried pods that are simply fried in lard or oil and eaten; green chile stew, which is virtually identical to the Hispanic version; green pumpkin stew, which is pumpkin stewed with corn, onion, green chiles and garlic; and red chile stew, which is usually made with pork.

Since meat was preserved in the old days by either salting or drying, an Indian favorite is beef or lamb jerky, which is often treated with chile powder. The jerky may be added to stews if fresh meat is not available.

The Spanish Contribution

The Old World meets the New and transforms the eating habits of the region

Imagine Southwestern cuisine without beef, lamb, pork, chicken, cilantro, cumin, limes, garlic, onions, wheat bread, rice, beer, and wine. That's where New World cooking would be without the Old. The Spanish colonists brought a new dimension to this ancient cuisine because the native peoples had never before experienced food sources such as cattle and wheat. The new foodstuffs merged with the old but did not overwhelm them. Rather, they were incorporated into the ancient techniques, and the result was a unique and highly spiced cuisine.

Dancers performing a traditional Spanish danza folklórica, *a Flamenco-style dance, at the Fiestas de Santa Fe, a three-day-long celebration that takes place every September.*

The Spaniards who first settled Santa Fe brought with them the seeds to plant the crops they needed as well as livestock. Since Santa Fe was the terminus of the 1,500-mile-long *Camino Real* (Royal Road) from Mexico City, it became a trading center and both the beginning and the end for caravans of wagons. The Plaza in Santa Fe was where the wagons unloaded, and vigorous trading was done in foodstuffs.

The primary crops of the colonists were corn and squash. Historian Marc Simmons wrote about the early Spanish agriculture: "Other field crops included the *frijol* bean, horsebean, peas, squashes and pumpkins, melons, chile, tobacco, and cotton. Only a limited variety of garden vegetables seem to have been cultivated in the later Colonial period. Onions and garlic were regarded as staples in the diet, but other things, such as cucumbers, lettuce, beets, and the small husk-tomato, are mentioned in the documents only rarely. The potato was practically unknown."

The first and most important Old World influences were meats and grains. "Wherever Spaniards went, they took their livestock with them," notes John C. Super, an expert on colonial Latin American history. "Pigs, sheep, and cattle were as much a part of the conquest as Toledo steel and fighting mastiffs."

Indeed they were. In fact, the introduction of livestock was so successful that the animals thrived even when they escaped into the wild. Within a century after the arrival of Columbus, the estimated New World population of cattle was 800,000, and of sheep, an astonishing 4.6 million. Sheep were introduced in 1598 by Capitán General Juan de Oñate. By the 1880s, there were millions of sheep in New Mexico and about 500,000 a year were exported. Today, the number of sheep produced remains at about half a million. With all that additional meat available, no wonder the cuisines of the Americas changed radically. Beef was readily added to such dishes as enchiladas, while pork was a favorite for *carne adovada,* the baked, chile-marinated dish. Domestic fowl such as chickens added diversity as their meat was incorporated into the corn cuisine of Santa Fe.

Wheat was also instrumental in changing the ways the Native Americans cooked by offering an alternative to corn for making the most basic food of all: bread. It was planted in such abundance throughout Mexico that by the middle of the sixteenth century, it was more common in the New World than in Spain, where wheat supplies had dropped and the people were eating rye bread. In New Mexico, wheat tortillas eventually became as popular as those made with corn.

It is not generally known that New Mexico and El Paso are the two oldest wine-producing regions in the United States. A Franciscan friar, Augustín Rodríguez, is credited with bringing grape vines to southern New Mexico in 1580, about a hundred years before the friars in California planted their vineyards. By 1662, priests of the Mesilla Valley in southern New Mexico were regularly producing sacramental wine for Mass.

Making ristras, *strings of chile peppers, by hand at the Rancho de las Golondrinas, which was a stopping place for caravans from Mexico and is now a living history museum.*

It should be remembered that most of the Hispanic population of Santa Fe is the result of the early Spanish immigration from Mexico, and not from later Mexican immigration. The descendants of the early settlers have lived and prospered in the region for about four hundred years, and today, together with all other Hispanics, make up approximately 40 percent of the population. Thus the Hispanics of New Mexico refer to their Spanish heritage.

Hot, Hotter, Hottest

The glorious chile pepper comes in many varieties, each with its own shape, size color and flavor

Surprisingly, the now ubiquitous chile peppers are not native to New Mexico at all, but were introduced from Central America by Spanish conquistadors in the sixteenth century. According to one member of the Antonio Espejo expedition of 1582–83, Baltasar Obregón, "They have no chile, but the natives were given some seed to plant." Even by 1601, chiles were still not on the list of Indian crops, according to colonist Francisco de Valverde, who also complained that mice were a pest that ate chile pods off the plants in the field.

Right: *Capsaicinoids, the heat-producing substances in chile peppers, can be seen here as golden droplets in the center below the seeds.* ***Opposite:*** *Chiles come in a wide range of colors, shapes, sizes and levels of heat. This photograph shows a small selection of that vast array.*

After the Spanish began settlement of the area, the cultivation of chile peppers developed rapidly, and soon they were grown all over New Mexico. It is likely that many different varieties were cultivated, including early forms of jalapeños, *serranos, anchos,* and *pasillas.* But one variety that adapted particularly well to New Mexico was a long green chile that turned red in the fall. Formerly called Anaheim because of its transfer to California around 1900, the New Mexican chiles were cultivated for hundreds of years in the region with such dedication that several distinct varieties developed. These varieties, Chimayó and Española, are still planted today in the fields they were grown in centuries ago; they are a small, distinct part of the tons of chile pods produced each year in New Mexico.

In 1846, William Emory, Chief Engineer of the Army's Topographic Unit, was surveying the New Mexico landscape and its customs. He described a meal eaten in Bernalillo, just north of Albuquerque: "Roast chicken, stuffed with onions; then mutton, boiled with onions; then followed various other dishes, all dressed with the everlasting onion; and the whole terminated by chile, the glory of New Mexico."

Emory went on to relate his experience with chiles: "Chile the Mexicans consider the chef-d'oeuvre of the cuisine, and seem really to revel in it; but the first mouthful brought the tears trickling down my cheeks, very much to the amusement of the spectators with their leather-lined throats. It was red pepper, stuffed with minced meat."

Las Cruces in southern New Mexico is well known for its bountiful chile harvest.

The earliest cultivated chiles in New Mexico were smaller than today's; indeed, they were (and still are, in some cases) considered a spice. But as the varieties developed and the size of the pods grew, the food value of chiles became evident. There was just one problem—the many sizes and shapes of the chile peppers made it very difficult for farmers to determine which chile they were growing from year to year. And there was no way to tell how large or how hot the pods might be until modern horticultural techniques produced more standardized chiles.

Today, New Mexico is by far the largest commercial producer of chile peppers in the United States, with about 35,000 acres under cultivation. All the primary dishes in New Mexican cuisine contain chile peppers: sauces, stews, *carne adovada,* enchiladas, tamales, and many vegetable dishes. The intense use of chiles as a food rather than just as a spice or condiment is what differentiates New Mexican cuisine from that of Texas or Arizona. In neighboring states chile powders are used as a seasoning for beef broth or chicken broth–based "chili gravies," which are thickened with flour or cornstarch before being added to, say, enchiladas. In New Mexico the sauces are made from pure chiles and are thickened by reducing the crushed or pureed pods. New Mexico chile *sauces* are cooked and pureed, while *salsas* use fresh, uncooked ingredients. Debates rage over whether tomatoes should be used in cooked sauces such as red chile sauce, but traditional cooked red sauces do *not* contain tomatoes, though uncooked salsas do.

Chile peppers have become the de facto state symbol. Houses are adorned with strings of dried red chiles, called *ristras.* Images of the pods are emblazoned on signs, T-shirts, coffee mugs, hats and even underwear. In the late summer and early fall, the rich aroma of roasting chiles fills the air all over the state. "*A la primera cocinera se le va un chile entero,*" goes one old Spanish *dicho* (saying): "To the best lady cook goes the whole chile." And the chile pepper is the single most important food in New Mexican cuisine.

The Arrival of the Anglos

New flavors travel to the Southwest along the Santa Fe Trail

Following Mexico's independence in 1821 and the opening of the Santa Fe Trail from Missouri, Santa Fe saw more and more trading (which had been prohibited by Spain, necessitating smuggling), and soon it was the terminus of two major trade routes from the east and the south. After Santa Fe fell to the Americans in 1846, the area really opened up as goods flooded in from the east.

Imported grains such as wheat became readily available with the arrival of the railroads. These grains were grown mostly on the eastern plains. However, imported flour was available, and corn was raised in small plots by both Hispanics and Native Americans. Agriculture was so primitive in the region that one critic, Antonio Barreiro, wrote in 1832: "Agriculture is utterly neglected, for the inhabitants of this country do not sow any amount, as they might do to great profit without any doubt. They sow barely what they consider necessary for their maintenance for part of the year, and the rest of the year they are exposed to a thousand miseries."

Wagon trains bringing goods from the eastern states, as well as luxuries from Europe, began making regular trips across the plains from Missouri in the 1820s. The momentous opening of the Sante Fe Trail is reenacted each year.

One such misery was described by Susan Magoffin, the teenaged bride of American trader and agent Samuel Magoffin. In her diary she describes her first taste of New Mexican green chile stew in 1846: "Oh how my heart sickened to say nothing of my stomach . . . [from] a mixture of meat, chilly verde & onions boiled together completing course No. 1. . . . There were a few mouthfuls taken, for I could not eat a dish so strong, and unaccustomed to my palate." However, she did become accustomed to spicy food and even wrote a "cookery book" so that her friends in the States (New Mexico was still a territory, of course) could experience New Mexican cuisine.

By 1846, champagne and oysters were available, and flour for making bread sold for $2.50 per *fanega.* If that sounds expensive, know that a *fanega* was 144 pounds. About this time, a Lieutenant James Abert was traveling extensively throughout New Mexico. Later, in his book *Through the Country of the Comanche Indians,* he described the market at Santa Fe: "The markets have . . . great quantities of 'Chile

Colorado' and 'verde,' 'cebollas' or onions, 'sandias' or watermelons, 'huevos' or eggs, 'uvas' or grapes, and 'pinones,' nuts of the pine tree."

Prices were relatively high. Corn was two dollars a bushel, beef and mutton eight to ten cents a pound, sugar and coffee were twenty-five cents a pound, and tea was very expensive at $1.25 a pound. About this time, W. W. H. Davis traveled to Santa Fe and sampled the native cuisine. In his book, *El Gringo,* he described his encounter: "The meal was a true Mexican dinner, and a fair sample of the style of living among the better class of people. The advance guard in the course of the dishes was boiled mutton and beans, the meat being young and tender, and well flavored. These were followed by a *sui generis* soup, different from any thing of the kind it had been my fortune to meet with before. It was filled with floating balls about the size of a musket bullet, which appeared to be a compound of flour and meat. Next came mutton stewed in *chile* (red peppers), the dressing of which was about the color of blood, and almost as hot as so much molten lead."

After mentioning the *albóndigas* soup and the mutton, Davis described the standard beans, tortillas, and *atole* (a corn drink) and then commented on chile: "Besides those already enumerated, there are other dishes, some of which have come down from the ancient inhabitants of the country. The *chile* they use in various ways—green, or *verde,* and in its dried state, the former being made into a sort of salad, and is esteemed to be a great luxury."

The agricultural situation improved shortly after the U.S. Army raised its flag over Santa Fe's Palace of the Governors and New Mexico was opened up to further settlement by American pioneers. The introduction of modern tools and techniques and new crops such as apples, peas and melons helped the farmers greatly. By 1900, more than 5 million acres were under cultivation in New Mexico.

Santa Fe survived the Civil War without a scratch and did well under American control. Hotels and restaurants flourished with the coming of the railroad. Gradually, wheat crops surpassed corn crops in the state. However, wheat tortillas have not supplanted those made of corn; both are still equally popular.

Cattle had been introduced by Juan de Oñate but only assumed a significant role in New Mexico after the Civil War. By 1890, after the great cattle drives to the New Mexico gold mines to feed the miners, there were 1.34 million head of cattle in the state. Remarkably, the figure nearly a hundred years later (1988) was almost identical: 1.32 million head.

After the Homestead Act of 1862 and the arrival of the railroad between 1879 and 1882, settlers from the eastern United States flooded into the state. With the advent of the railroad came the first railroad restaurants, the Harvey House chain. New Mexico boasted sixteen of these establishments, including five that were the grandest of the system: Montezuma and Castañeda in Las Vegas, La Fonda in Santa Fe, Alvarado in Albuquerque, and El Navajo in Gallup. Harvey hired young women between the ages of eighteen and thirty to be his hostesses, and they were quite an attraction on the Western frontier, where women were scarce. The humorist Will Rogers once said, "Fred Harvey kept the West in food and wives."

The Harvey Houses attempted to bring "civilized" food to the frontier, and early menus reveal dishes like chicken croquettes, baron of beef, turkey stuffed with oysters, vermicelli with cheese à la Italian, and the ever delectable calf's brains scrambled with ranch eggs. "Mexican" food was considered too "native" for travelers and rarely appeared on upscale hotel and restaurant menus.

A parade in downtown Santa Fe circa 1932. The large building on the left is La Fonda hotel, built in 1922 and still standing in the same spot today.

The railroads brought the settlers, and these pioneers brought new food crops. At first, vegetables such as tomatoes, asparagus, cabbage, carrots, lettuce, onions and peas were produced in home gardens on a small scale, but when extensive irrigation facilities were constructed in the early twentieth century, commercial vegetable production began.

During the years following World War I, Santa Fe began to emerge from obscurity as the city—and the rest of the state—was discovered by artists such as Peter Hurd and Georgia O'Keeffe, authors such as Willa Cather and D. H. Lawrence, and other prominent sculptors, poets, photographers and musicians. The high concentration of artists in the city, combined with Santa Fe's tradition as an Indian trading center, produced one of the top art markets in the world. More than 150 galleries (concentrated around the Plaza and along Canyon Road) now feature local as well as international artists, and special events such as Indian Market in mid-August ensure that the ancient artistic traditions are kept alive.

In the decades after World War I, the cuisines of Santa Fe, however, remained fairly segregated: an Indian-Hispanic hybrid cuisine served in the pueblos; hotels offered mostly standard meat and potatoes eastern-style; and the traditional New Mexican chile-based cuisine was served in Hispanic houses and restaurants. But major culinary changes would occur as Santa Fe became one of the top ten tourist destinations in the country.

Celebrations and Festivals

The many feasts of life in Santa Fe each seem to have their own celebratory foods

Santa Feans love to party, and the entire year seems to revolve around the many fiestas—one after another. Even calling these celebrations markets doesn't prevent people from partying.

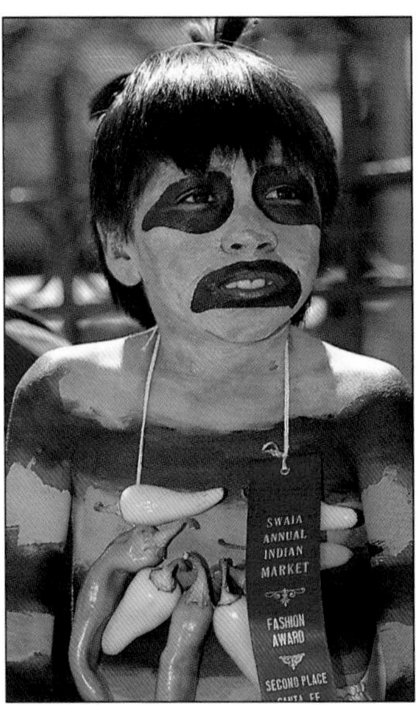

A young Hopi boy in the traditional costume of the koshare, *or clown, during Santa Fe's Indian Market. At Hopi feast days children often dress as* koshares *and cause mischief.*

Spanish Market, held during the last weekend in July for more than forty-five years, showcases the arts and crafts of New Mexico's Hispanic artisans. There is the Traditional Spanish Market, held on the Plaza, and the Contemporary Spanish Market, held in the courtyard of the Palace of the Governors. The crafts sold include *santos* (carved wooden saints), tinwork, embroidery, jewelry, weaving and handmade furniture

Indian Market, held around the Plaza during a weekend in mid-August for more than seventy-five years, is probably the finest single show of Indian arts and crafts in the United States. Collectors travel from all over the world to this event, which features only Indian-made arts and crafts. As with Spanish Market, numerous food booths featuring the local street fare of tacos, tostadas and burritos are also set up.

The Santa Fe Wine and Chile Festival is held in mid-September, and the events take place in various restaurants and cooking schools. A grand tasting is held in a tent in the parking lot of a downtown hotel and features traditional and innovative food prepared by Santa Fe's best restaurants, and wines from New Mexico, Texas and California wineries.

One of the largest celebrations in Santa Fe is Fiesta de Santa Fe, which was established in 1712 by Don Diego de Vargas to commemorate the reoccupation of New Mexico by the Spanish. It begins the Friday after Labor Day in Fort Marcy Park with the burning of Zozobra, a forty-foot-tall effigy representing Old Man Gloom. Afterward, the party moves to the Plaza and downtown area for two more days of parades, dancing, singing, religious processions, and booths filled with arts, crafts and traditional food. The best time to visit is during a feast day, for you can be sure that a ceremony or dance will take place. Of special fun are the grab or throw days. Many Native Americans are named for

Catholic saints, and on each saint's day, all pueblo members with that name go up on the roof and throw something down to the crowd that travels from house to house. Sweets such as commercial candy, apples, prizes, or even small plastic trash cans are among the items that get thrown. Historically, water would be flung from gourds to encourage rain, and although it is still done, children seem to prefer water balloons to gourds! You may get wet, but you'll have a good time.

At the end of August, the height of the tourist season in Santa Fe, large crowds mingle with Native American artists from all over the country at the Indian Market.

During the feast days at the Indian pueblos, tourists are welcome during most of the ceremonies and dances and may even be invited to join in. However, there is a definite etiquette to be observed. Enter a home by invitation only, and if invited to eat (which is common) don't refuse and don't linger, as others will be invited to take your place. Limit your questions—asking too many will be viewed as inconsiderate. And don't walk across the plaza or dance area, look into kivas or talk to dancers during the ceremonies; remember that these are religious shrines and activities.

It is always best to check with the tribal or tourist office before wandering into a pueblo. They can steer you to craftspeople and places of interest and inform you of the particular rules governing that pueblo. Always respect Indian traditions when you're on their land; it is a sovereign nation, and you are subject to their laws and regulations.

Other special events in Santa Fe include Rodeo de Santa Fe, which began in the 1940s and has steadily grown into a popular regional competition. It happens in early July, and between three and five hundred cowboys compete in riding, roping and racing events. The Santa Fe Festival of the Arts is held in October, and history buffs will enjoy the Mountain Man Rendezvous and Buffalo Roast held in mid-August on the Plaza.

The Christmas season in New Mexico always brings its distinctive sights, aromas and tastes. The traditional colors of the season are evident in the red and green New Mexican chiles; the aroma of burning piñon pine permeates the air. The Spanish

Right: *La Entrada, a reenactment of the reconquest of Santa Fe by Don Diego de Vargas after the Pueblo Indians revolted against the Spanish, is a popular spectacle during the Fiestas de Santa Fe, which has been celebrated since 1712.* **Opposite:** Farolitos *light the Christ child's way through Santa Fe at Christmastime. These lanterns are called* luminarias *in Albuquerque, but don't try calling them that in Santa Fe.*

brought Christmas to the Southwest about four hundred years ago, but the Pueblo Indians were already celebrating this time of the year with a number of feast days. After the harvest was stored for the winter, dances were performed both to give thanks for the bounty and to apologize for the necessity of having to hunt for winter food. These traditions continue to this day.

Probably no other image symbolizes the Christmas season in New Mexico more than the *luminarias* that line walkways and outline buildings and houses throughout the state. Originally, little crisscross fires of piñon wood were lit on Christmas Eve to light the Christ child's way. With the advent of the square-bottomed brown paper bag, the bonfires were replaced with a votive candle anchored in sand in the bag—and the *farolito* (little lantern) was born. Whether called *luminarias* or *farolitos,* they are traditionally lit only on December 24, *la noche buena;* and with most electric lights turned off, they weave a quiet, soft spell.

Many of the tastes of the season are prepared from recipes handed down from generation to generation. These recipes incorporate a mixture of cultures—Indian, Spanish, and Anglo—and utilize locally available foodstuffs, including corn for flour or dried for use in stews, whole pods of chile from the strings of *ristras,* and meat from livestock that could not be kept over the winter. Stews like *posole* were kept on the stove to feed friends stopping by after Mass or for hosting neighborhood *posadas,* Spanish plays enacting Mary and Joseph's search for an inn. Many of these traditions continue today in New Mexico homes. For example, it is not unusual for spectators attending Indian dances at a pueblo on Christmas Eve to be invited into a home for tamales, a bowl of *posole* or green chile stew, or even some *carne adovada.* Dessert would be *flan* (custard), *natillas* (soft custard) or *biscochitos* (anise-flavored shortbread cookies). It would be impolite to refuse the invitation to dine, since it is a part of the New Mexican Christmas tradition for everyone who stops by.

Dining Out in Santa Fe

A new generation of chefs reinvent the traditional cuisine while adding quite a few new flavors of their own

Within a few of blocks of the Plaza in Santa Fe, foodies can indulge every gastronomic whim imaginable. Want to buy the hottest salsa known to man? Like some to-die-for blue corn enchiladas with delicious red chile? Care to taste some New Mexican wines and beers? Need a *ristra* for your front porch? It's all here in Santa Fe.

There are probably more fine restaurants per capita in Santa Fe than anywhere else in the United States, and this is undoubtedly the result of tourism.

As is true of New Mexico in general, people living in and visiting the City Different love their food spicy hot. In fact, a study done a few years ago determined that Santa Fe is the fiery food capital of the country. Despite the spiciness of the Santa Fe food, visitors should note that there is a wide variety of cuisines available to sample because Santa Fe attracts great culinary artists as well as great visual artists. There isn't space here to mention all of the city's great restaurants, so we have described only our personal favorites.

Right: *Twilight outside Cafe Pasqual's, one of Santa Fe's best-known eateries.* ***Opposite:*** *The garden courtyard outside La Casa Sena provides a quiet dining spot for residents and visitors.*

Travel back in time as you reach the end of the Santa Fe Trail at **La Fonda** hotel and restaurant (100 E. San Francisco Street), a mainstay in Santa Fe for three hundred years. Although the current structure is only eighty years old, it is filled with the charm of Old Santa Fe and features thick adobe walls, high ceilings, carved wood furniture, stone floors, and big inviting fireplaces. The restaurant is in an atrium with painted windows and turn-of-the-century art, including works by legendary artist Georgia O'Keeffe.

The menu is inspired by the cuisines of Old Mexico and Spain and contains items such as Grilled Quail Breast with Ancho Chile Glaze served in a Sweet Potato Taco, Wild Boar Carnitas, and rattlesnake dishes.

From artists to outlaws, much of Santa Fe's history has been witnessed at the bar of **El Farol** (808 Canyon Road), a popular social spot for locals since 1835. The stories say that it was the scene of many gunfights, and in the 1950s, famed artist Alfred Morang paid his tab

by painting a mural on one of the walls. Hidden underneath paneling for a number of years, his work has now been restored and continues to be a popular attraction. The fare is traditional Spanish, and the specialties are *tapas* (they even have a designated Tapas Room), *paella* and Spanish wines.

The tradition of great restaurants in Santa Fe during the modern era was born more than forty-five years ago when Rosalea Murphy opened **The Pink Adobe** (406 Old Santa Fe Trail). As Rosalea recalls, when "the Pink" first opened, Santa Fe was not the tourist mecca it is today, but rather a "lazy, sleepy town." She served twenty-five-cent "Pink Dobeburgers," then imported chicken enchiladas from Mexico, and eventually became the first chef in Santa Fe to serve seafood. Today, the restaurant is located in a former barracks for Spanish soldiers, Barrio de Analco, one of the oldest parts of Santa Fe. Despite its name, the Pink Adobe is no longer pink but rather a shade of sandstone. Santa Fe's Historical Design Review Board has refused to allow the restaurant to be painted its original color because, according to the board, pink is not an earth tone. During a hearing on the issue, Rosalea presented several samples of pink rocks collected in the desert and mountains around Santa Fe, but the board still refused.

Coyote Cafe owner Mark Miller, who is today renowned as one of America's leading chefs.

The **Coyote Cafe** (132 West Water Street) offers a truly unique dining experience because anthropologist-turned-chef Mark Miller presents a different menu each day, re-creating Southwestern and Latin American dishes that predate the arrival of Europeans. It is difficult to suggest any one particular menu item because they change so much, but some past menus have included Barbecued Duck Crepas, layered corn crepes with roast duck, barbecue sauce, and corn chile relish; and Red Chile Quail, fresh Texas bobwhite quail marinated in dried chiles and wild mushrooms.

"My café is small but lively," says Katharine Kagel, chef-owner of **Cafe Pasqual's** (121 Don Gaspar Avenue), which has been in business since 1979. Located one block from the historic Plaza, the café serves the food of New and Old Mexico, as well as New American Cuisine. During the day, the atmosphere is informal, but the mood changes at dinnertime when the white tablecloths come out and the wine service begins. Signature dishes include Huevos Motuleños, a Yucatán egg dish, and Chicken Mole Presciliano, a Pueblo-style family recipe made with twenty different ingredients. The café also boasts an art gallery that features Mexican murals, traditional Apache cookware, and jewelry.

The three cultures of Santa Fe come together in the food and the architecture of **Inn of the Anasazi** (113 Washington Avenue), where Native American spirituality, Mexican flair, and European practicality define the experience. Diners can settle in on cozy *bancos* to warm their bones by the fire and their insides with cutting-edge dishes like Grilled Tortilla and Lime Soup with Barbecued Yellow Tomato Salsa and Cilantro Corn Oil, a popular appetizer that has been on the menu since the award-winning restaurant opened in 1991.

La Casa Sena (125 East Palace Avenue) was expanded from a small house to a thirty-three-room adobe hacienda in 1868 by a prominent Santa Fe family. The courtyard, once a feeding ground for goats, is now one of the city's most beautiful outdoor dining spots. The restaurant opened in 1983 and serves innovative dishes such as Grilled Pepita Crusted Salmon with Ancho Chile Hollandaise and Goat Cheese Epazote Quesadilla.

Serving traditional northern New Mexico cuisine, **Maria's New Mexican Kitchen** (555 West Cordova Road) was originally a take-out place started in the early 1950s by Maria, the young wife of a local politician. After several years she sold it, and it has grown since. The menu includes many traditional dishes. Owner Al Lucero says that his place was the first to introduce fajitas to Santa Fe back in 1985. However, margaritas, over seventy-five of them, are Maria's main claim to fame. They are made with only the best authentic tequilas and are hand-shaken never stirred.

The **Santacafé** (231 Washington Street), a "Southwest American Bistro" in a 150-year-old building, has been open since 1983 and is a local favorite for its innovative menu and celebrity-watching opportunities. Its decor is not traditional Southwestern but rather stark minimalist, with bare off-white walls. The signature dish is Crispy Calamari with Lime Dipping Sauce, and the menu includes Grilled Rack of Lamb with Pasilla Chile Sauce and Roasted Corn–Shiitake Mushroom Salsa. It has been named a top-rated restaurant by Zagat's guide.

Since 1989, the **Santa Fe School of Cooking** (116 West San Francisco Street) has defined traditional New Mexican cooking and has set the tone for contemporary Southwest cuisine with dishes like Lime-Marinated Grilled Salmon with Ginger-Lime Butter. "We mirror Santa Fe," says Susan Curtis, founder of the school. Many Santa Fe chefs have taught or studied here, and instruction is open to all.

Paul's Restaurant of Santa Fe (72 West Marcy Street) is an intimate place that incorporates the best of all worlds, from its folksy yet modern atmosphere to its eclectic cuisine. "We don't follow trends," says owner Paul Hunsicker, who opened the restaurant in 1990. His menu combines flavors from around the world in dishes like Baked Salmon in a Pecan Herb Crust and Red Chile Duck Wontons.

The many innovations of the new Southwestern chefs, while surprising, are fully in keeping with the past. In New Mexico, the traditional cuisine based on corn, beans, squash, and chile will probably be cooked for centuries to come. But this doesn't mean that it has to be static. And today's chefs are creating exciting new food by blending the ideas of other cultures with the fundamentals of Southwestern cookery and ingredients in wonderful new ways.

Part Two: The Santa Fe Kitchen

A guide to essential utensils, cooking methods and ingredients

Despite the food of Santa Fe seeming to be quite exotic, the equipment necessary to cook it is not strange at all. The traditional utensils, originally from Mexico, are all but obsolete in these days of premade tortillas and electrical appliances. In earlier times, a ***metlapil***, a cylindrical stone, would be rolled on a ***metate***, a flat, rectangular stone (see page 93), to grind the corn kernels for tortillas. After the corn was ground and a *masa* (corn dough) made, corn tortillas would be prepared with a rolling pin, but the Spanish developed the first wooden **tortilla presses** to make the process easier. Presses were hand carved from mesquite or made of metal. Now more commonly made of cast aluminum or iron, a press consists of two plates, a hinge, and a handle that you press to flatten and shape the ball of *masa*. Wheat tortillas have always been prepared with a rolling pin and fingertips. After flattening, the tortillas would be cooked on a ***comal*** (griddle).

A ***molcajete y tejolote***—a volcanic-rock mortar and pestle—would be used to grind spices or to make salsas for tortilla dishes. A ***molinillo***, a short stick with indentations in the bulb at its tip, was used (and still is), to prepare frothy hot chocolate.

In the modern Santa Fe kitchen, a food processor or blender has taken over the tasks of the *metates* and *molcajetes*, and a *comal* has been replaced by a **griddle** or **cast-iron skillet**. Casseroles have replaced ***cazuelas***, the glazed earthenware pots ubiquitious in Southwestern antique shops.

A **spice mill** is handy to have not only for grinding spices but for grinding chiles into powder. When you grind chiles, you may want to wear a paint mask to avoid breathing in the powder. You will need airtight containers to store ground chile powders.

For making chile sauce, an eight-quart **Dutch oven** is recommended. A **steamer** is useful for cooking tamales. A **charcoal** or **gas grill** is useful for roasting chiles and to grill meat, although chiles can be roasted in a conventional oven or toaster oven as well.

A **deep fryer** is ideal for making *sopaipillas*, the puffed-up bread. A heavy saucepan can be substituted if you do not have a deep fryer.

Opposite: *The kitchen of the Martinez Hacienda, a restored Spanish Colonial adobe house dating from circa 1804, which originally belonged to a mayor of Taos.* ***Left:*** *These dippers are examples of the exquisitely detailed pottery of the Mimbres (left) and Tanto (right) peoples, who lived in southern New Mexico and Arizona. The Mimbres vanished after about 1150* A.D.

Making Corn Tortillas

Tlaxcallim (corn tortillas) were the principal food of both the Mayas and the Aztecs as early as 10,000 B.C. Both cultures worshiped corn, and the Mayas believed that humans were created from corn dough (*masa*). Corn tortillas are made in much the same way today as they have been for centuries. Dried corn kernels are briefly cooked in a solution of water and unslaked lime (calcium hydroxide), or "builder's lime," to remove their tough skin and soften them enough to grind. The resulting *nixtamal* is combined with water to form *masa*.

Tortillas can only be made from *masa;* cornmeal will not work. If you cannot purchase ready-to-use *masa, masa harina,* which is dehydrated *nixtamal,* is available in many grocery stores alongside the flour or from a number of mail-order sources.

There are a variety of ways to form corn tortillas. The most difficult method is by hand. A flattened ball of *masa* about an inch in diameter is worked between the hands in a rapid, smooth motion. Mastering this art is not as easy as it looks and takes a lot of practice!

To use a tortilla press, make the dough using the recipe on page 106. Once your *masa* balls are ready, cover the bottom plate of the press with a piece of heavy plastic wrap or wax paper that is a little larger than the press. Place the ball on the press a little off center, toward the hinge. Cover the dough with another piece of plastic, close the press, and push the handle down hard. Open the press, peel off the top piece of plastic, place the tortilla plastic side up on one hand, remove the remaining plastic, and gently roll the tortilla onto a heated *comal* or skillet to cook. Don't try to peel the tortilla off the plastic—trust us, it won't work.

If you don't have a press, you can roll out the *masa* between two pieces of plastic wrap with a rolling pin. Remove the plastic as described above.

Step 1: *Cover the bottom plate with plastic wrap, position the ball of* masa *and cover it with another sheet of wrap.*

Step 2: *Lower the handle of the press and apply firm pressure.*

Step 3: *Open the press, lift off the top plastic, pick up the tortilla and place it on your palm, plastic side up. Peel away the remaining sheet of plastic.*

Making Flour Tortillas

The Spanish name *tortilla* comes from the word *torta,* which means "round cake," an apt description of this flat, unleavened bread. When the Spanish brought wheat to the Western Hemisphere, the flour tortilla (*tortilla de harina*) was born.

Flour tortillas are popular in the northern states of Mexico and in the southwestern United States, and they vary in size and thickness. Those made in California and Arizona are much thinner than those made in New Mexico. Unlike corn tortillas, flour tortillas contain fat. Lard is traditionally used, which tends to result in a crumbly tortilla, but those made with vegetable shortening can sometimes be bland. A combination of both produces a good tortilla.

Flour tortillas aren't formed by hand or in a press—they must be rolled because of the gluten in the wheat. A small rolling pin is best because it applies less pressure and results in a lighter tortilla. The best and least expensive rolling pin, and the one most often found in Mexico, is simply a length of broom handle. You can also use a wooden dowel from the hardware store. Whichever you choose, be sure to wash it well before you use it.

You don't roll a tortilla as you do a pie crust. Instead, lightly flour a smooth surface and, using your fingers, pinch out pieces of dough about an inch and a half in diameter. Then, flatten each piece of dough and form it into a circle. With the rolling pin, roll a circle of dough front and back and then rotate it a quarter turn. Flip the tortilla over every few rotations and roll it until it is very round and thin. Once you have completed this first step, drape the tortilla over one hand and gradually stretch the dough out from around the edges with the other. This too takes practice. The finished tortilla should be seven or eight inches in diameter.

Fry the raw tortilla in a heated comal or skillet with a little vegetable oil until it is firm, turning it only once. If it puffs up, flatten it with a spatula.

Although the best tortillas are fresh and warm, you can store them in the refrigerator for up to a week or freeze them. Cold tortillas need to be warmed in order to soften them, and there are a number of ways to do so. To steam them, put a half inch of water in a steamer and heat two tortillas at a time for 1 minute—no longer, or they will become soft and soggy—and then let them stand for 15 minutes. You can also cover a stack of tortillas with foil and heat them for 15 minutes in a 325°F oven. For faster results, wrap them in a towel and microwave them for 20 to 30 seconds on full power. If you have a gas stove, the quickest and easiest way is to heat them for a couple of seconds on each side over an open burner.

Preparing Chile Peppers

Travelers to New Mexico in the late summer and early fall are treated to the sight of forty-pound sacks of potent green chiles at roadside stands and are often tempted to buy one. But then what do you do with them?

New Mexican chiles are usually blistered and peeled before being used in recipes. Blistering the chile is the process of roasting the fresh pods to the point at which the tough transparent skin separates from the meat of the chile so it can be removed. This roasting is what gives New Mexican chile sauces their distinctive burnt, smoky flavor. Fresh, firm chiles are the easiest to peel. As chiles age, the flesh becomes soft and the skin starts to wrinkle and tends to fall apart during processing. Should you have to use one with a slightly wrinkled skin, rub it with a little vegetable oil before blistering.

To roast and peel chiles, first cut a small slit close to the stem end so that the steam can escape and the pod won't explode. The chiles can be placed on a baking sheet and put directly under the broiler, or on a screen on the stovetop. They can also be plunged into hot cooking oil to loosen the skin.

Our favorite method, which involves meditation with a six-pack of Santa Fe Pale Ale, is to place the pods on a charcoal grill about five or six inches from the coals. Blisters will soon indicate that the skin is separating; be sure to turn them as they cook so that the chiles are blistered all over, or they will not peel properly. Although the chiles may burn slightly, take care that they do not blacken (they will be nearly impossible to peel).

Immediately wrap the chiles in damp paper towels and place them in a plastic bag to steam for 10 to 15 minutes. The best way to avoid chile burns from the capsaicin that gives chiles their heat is to wear rubber gloves during the peeling process. Remove the skin, stem and seeds of each pod and chop the flesh coarsely. Place the chopped chile in plastic ice cube trays and freeze it solid. Pop out the cubes and place them in Ziploc freezer bags: you'll have easy access to whatever amount of chile is needed for a recipe. The taste of Santa Fe will keep in your freezer for at least a year.

Dried chile pods should be stored in airtight containers to prevent insect damage, but of course many people buy the long strings, or *ristras,* of red chiles and simply pluck them off as needed. But *ristras* are designed for dry climates and suffer in excess humidity. The best storage for dried pods is in self-sealing plastic bags in the freezer. Some sauces require that you remove the seeds and membranes of dried chiles and soak them in warm water before using them.

ROASTING CHILES

Step 1: *Make a slit at the top of each chile for the steam to escape. Roast over an open flame, turning until the skin blisters on all sides.*

Step 2: *Wrap the blistered chiles in a damp cloth for a few minutes. The steam will loosen the skin.*

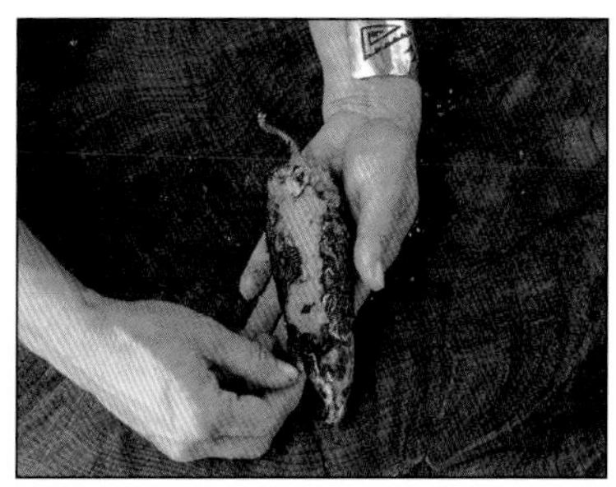

Step 3: *Gently peel the skin off. If you have sensitive skin you may want to wear gloves to do this.*

SEEDING AND SOAKING DRIED CHILES

Step 1: *Cut open the dried chiles lengthwise. If you plan to stuff them, make a slit and empty them through it.*

Step 2: *Remove the seeds and the tough, white membranes.*

Step 3: *Soak them in warm water only long enough to soften them, about 15 to 20 minutes.*

Grinding them into powders is an efficient way to store chiles in small spaces, but be sure to keep them in airtight containers away from sunlight, to prevent oxidation and fading. To make chile powder, the pods must be thoroughly dried until they are brittle. Use a microwave on low power or a 200°F oven for a few hours. The next step is to grind the chiles into powder. Be sure to wear a paint mask for at least some protection against inhaling the pungent capsaicin fumes. Using a spice mill or coffee grinder, grind the chiles to the desired consistency. They may be ground to a fine powder called *molido* or be coarsely ground with some of the seeds, which is called *quebrado*.

1. piñon nuts 2. lentils 3. epazote 4. mexican oregano 5. atole 6. canela (cinnamon) 7. piloncillo (brown sugar) 8. posole 9. manzanilla (camomile) 10. crushed chiles 11. red chile powder 12. pinto beans 13. chicos 14. coriander seeds 15. green chile powder 16. black beans 17. blue corn 18. anasazi beans

Santa Fe Ingredients

A few notes on the usual and unusual products in every well-stocked New Mexican kitchen

Here are the essentials for preparing Santa Fe dishes. Call this number to receive a free list of sources for ingredients: (800) 526-2778.

ACHIOTE: The orange-colored seeds of the tropical annatto tree that are used as a coloring agent and a seasoning.

ANISEED: The licorice-flavored spice that is used to make *bizcochitos* (a type of cookie).

BEANS: Most beans are varieties of the kidney bean, *Phaseolus vulgaris.* By far the most popular bean in New Mexico is the **pinto bean**, but other varieties are slowly being adopted into the Santa Fe cuisine. The pinto bean is so named because of its brown-and-white "painted" appearance. It is boiled with spices and chiles and is often mashed and refried. The **black turtle bean** is a small black bean commonly used in Caribbean soups or stews. Sometimes it is refried. The **white Aztec bean**, native to the Southwest, is a large round white bean with a nutty flavor. The **New Mexican black appaloosa bean**, also native, is a spotted black-and-white bush bean that is often used in place of the pinto bean.

CHEESE: The American cheeses used most commonly in Santa Fe are Monterey jack, cheddar, and goat cheese. However, some Mexican cheeses are available, and the following are recommended. ***Adobera*** cheese, which is shaped like an adobe brick, looks and tastes like Monterey jack but holds its shape when heated. ***Asadero***, which means "broiler" or "roaster" cheese is from Coahuila. This mild, soft, often braided cheese is sold in tortilla-sized slices or wound into balls. ***Chihuahua*** is a mild, spongy, creamy, and pale yellow cheese that gets stringy when it is heated. It is also called ***queso menonita***. Substitute feta cheese if you can't obtain it. ***Fresco*** is a fresh, salty, crumbly white cheese served with salads and salsas. Also called ***queso blanco***, ***ranchero***, ***quesito***, and ***estilo casero***. Substitute feta if you can't obtain it.

CHORIZO: A spicy sausage made with ground pork, garlic, and red chile powder, it is sometimes placed in casings but most often is served crumbly. Substitute Italian sausage or any spicy pork sausage.

CILANTRO: An annual herb (*Coriandrum sativum*) with seeds that are known as coriander. The fresh leaves are commonly used in salsas and soups. Substitute Italian parsley, but the flavor is slightly different.

Epazote

Jicama

Nopales

Piloncillo

Pepitas

Piñon Nuts

Tomatillos

CORN: In the Santa Fe kitchen, three types of corn are used: yellow, white, and blue. Multicolored Indian corn is mostly used for decoration. Blue corn is particularly popular for its slightly nutty taste. The following products can be made from any of the three main varieties: ***Posole*** corn is corn kernels that have been treated with lime to remove their tough skin; it is then used in the pork and chile stew called *posole.* ***Chicos*** are dried corn kernels that are steamed and added to soups and stews. No lime is used in the process. **Corn husks**, softened in hot water, are used as a wrapping for tamales. **Cornmeal** is the coarsely ground dried corn for making cornbread. **Corn flour** is the finely ground, lime-treated dried corn in the dough called ***masa***.

CUMIN: *Comino* in Spanish, this is an annual herb (*Cuminum cyminum*) whose seeds (used whole or powdered) have a distinctive, musty odor. It is used to flavor sauces and main dishes.

EPAZOTE: Known as "Ambrosia" in English, this perennial herb (*Chenopodium ambrosioides*) is strong and bitter and is used primarily to flavor beans because it is said to aid in their digestion. It can be used either fresh or dry.

HUITLACOCHE: This is a fungus that grows on corn and is used like mushrooms in cooking. Also spelled Acuitlacoche.

JICAMA: A white tuber (*Pachyrhizus erosus*) shaped like a large, flattened top that is used in salads. An import from Mexico, it tastes like a cross between an apple and a potato.

JUNIPER BERRIES: Collected in the wild, these small blue berries add flavor to lamb and game dishes. They can be used fresh or dry.

MEXICAN CHOCOLATE: Chocolate with sugar and cinnamon that comes in pressed and scored cakes. It is used to make a frothy, rich hot chocolate and in baking. Ibarra is a good brand.

MEXICAN OREGANO: Actually, this is wild marjoram (*Lippia graveolens*), distinctly different from European or Greek oregano (*Origanum vulgare*). It can be used fresh or dry.

NOPALES: Spineless cactus leaves from the genus *Opuntia.* They are chopped or cut into strips and used fresh in salads or cooked as a vegetable. They have a slightly tart green bean flavor.

PEPITAS: Dried and roasted squash or pumpkin seeds; they are salted and eaten as a snack or used in chile sauces.

PILONCILLO: Unrefined sugar that is sold in cone shapes. It has a slight flavor of molasses and is primarily used in baking.

PIÑON NUTS: These are collected in the wild from pine cones of *Pinus edulis* and are used in desserts and main dishes.

QUELITES: Also called lamb's-quarters or wild spinach, this native plant is a green that is used in salads.

TOMATILLOS: The small green tomato relative, sometimes called *tomate verde*. They are tart and have a light brown outer covering, or husk, that must be removed before using. They should be firm; never use soft tomatillos.

A Guide to Chiles

There are so many different kinds of chiles that it can be hard to keep them straight. But the differences in flavor are so significant, that it's worth trying to learn to identify the important ones.

The principal chile peppers in Santa Fe cooking are the New Mexican varieties, called **Anaheims** in California. More than 35,000 acres are under cultivation in New Mexico. In their fresh form, they are called simply **green chiles**, and the pods are roasted and peeled before use. Fresh red pods can also be used in this manner. When dried, red chiles can be used whole or ground into powder. At flea markets and Santa Fe and Albuquerque you will find stands where farmers sell their own red and green chile powders, ground chipotle, and *ristras* of every size.

There are a number of varieties of New Mexican chiles, and all are readily available in Santa Fe. They range from the relatively mild **Big Jim, NuMex Joe E. Parker** and **No. 6-4** that are grown in the southern part of the state to the hotter northern varieties such as **Barker, Española** and **Velarde.** Incidentally, **Hatch chile** is not a variety but merely a geographical designation of the chile-growing region around Hatch, in the Rio Grande Valley of southern New Mexico.

In addition to the New Mexican varieties, many Mexican chiles appear in northern New Mexican cooking. They are easily obtained in markets, shops, and natural-food supermarkets. Each chile has an entirely different flavor profile, so don't substitute randomly. Appropriate substitutions are suggested.

The ***ancho*** is the dried form of the ***poblano.*** The fresh green pods range in length from three to six inches and in width from three to four inches. The fresh pods are roasted and peeled; then they are stuffed with meat, vegetables or cheese to make *chiles rellenos,* cut into strips, chopped, or sometimes ground into a powder. The reddish-brown *anchos* are usually toasted on a griddle and rehydrated before they are used. The *anchos* have a flavor that is often described as tasting like raisins. This variety is rather mild. *Pasilla* chiles may be substituted for *anchos* .

The spherical ***cascabel*** chile is about an inch and a half in diameter and is most frequently used in its dried form. When the chile is dry, the seeds rattle in the pod—accounting for its name, which translates roughly as "jingle bell." *Cascabels* are used in sauces and to spice up many other dishes, such as soups and stews. *Cascabels* have medium heat. Substitute *guajillo* chiles if you can't find *cascabels.*

Literally, a ***chipotle*** is any smoked chile, but the term generally refers to a jalapeño that has been partially dried in the sun and then smoked. Dark brown or red, about two inches long and an inch wide, they come in two forms: dried, or canned in an ***adobo* sauce**, which is a tomato-based sauce. Dried *chipotles* are rehydrated before use and are sometimes ground into powder. These chiles are moderately hot and have a wonderfully complex flavor. There is no real substitute for these smoked chiles.

The name ***de Árbol*** means "tree chile," an allusion to the appearance of the plant. About three inches long and three-eighths of an inch wide, the dried pods are used in cooked sauces of all kinds and are sometimes ground into a powder. The pods have medium heat. A good substitute is *mirasol.*

Similar in appearance to New Mexican varieties, ***guajillos*** are used mostly in their dry form. They are four to six inches long and about an inch and a half wide. The pods are orange-red, medium hot, and are used primarily in sauces. The substitute is dried red **New Mexican** chiles.

Grown in the Yucatán Peninsula, the lantern-shaped, orange ***habanero*** chiles are the hottest peppers in the world. The pods are about an inch and a half long and an inch wide and have a distinctive aroma that is fruity and apricotlike. They are used primarily in their fresh form in Mexico but also appear dried in the United States and Canada. The fresh pods are used extensively in salsas and other Yucatecan dishes. There is no real substitute for the flavor of fresh *habaneros*; use the hottest fresh chiles you can find, such as **cayenne** or **Thai**. For dried *habaneros*, substitute *piquín.*

Perhaps the most common chile in Mexico, the familiar **jalapeño** is one to two inches long and about three quarters of an inch wide. Unless they are smoked to create *chipotles,* jalapeños are used exclusively fresh in a great number of dishes. They have medium heat and are often found pickled in cans. To pickle them, they are sautéed with spices then covered with vinegar and stored in a dark place to develop the flavor. *Serranos* may be substituted.

The name ***mirasol*** means "looking at the sun," an allusion to the erect pods, which measure up to four inches long and are about three quarters of an inch wide. The medium-hot pods are used dried in sauces and meat dishes and are sometimes ground into powder. The substitute is *de Árbol.*

Fresh ***pasilla*** chiles are called ***chilacas*** and are used in a similar manner to New Mexican varieties or *poblanos.* When dried, the pods are five to six inches long and about an inch and a half wide. They are used in sauces and may be stuffed. The pods are mild and are sometimes ground into powder. As the name "little raisin" implies, the pods have a raisiny aroma and flavor. The substitute for *pasilla* is *ancho.*

The small, erect ***piquín*** pods are less than an inch long and a half inch wide; they usually resemble miniature bullets or peas. ***Chiltepíns*** were the only chile that the Native Americans cultivated in the wild before the arrival of the Spanish. They are spherical *piquíns* that measure about a quarter inch in diameter. Their name is believed to be derived from the Aztec words *chilli* and *tecpintl,* meaning "flea chile," an allusion to the *chiltepín*'s sharp bite. The pods of both are used in salsas, added to soups and stews, or ground into powder. They are hot to extremely hot. The substitute is dried *habanero.*

Both the red and green varieties of the ***serrano*** chile are used fresh. Measuring one to three inches long and a half inch wide, it is the chile of choice in Mexico for fresh salsas and has medium heat. The name means "mountain chile" or "highland chile." The *serrano* is often found pickled in cans. Jalapeño is a good substitute.

poblano
New Mexican (green)
New Mexican (red)
pasilla
ancho
serrano
jalapeño
yellow hot
chipotle
de Árbol
cayenne
Japones
habanero
piquín
chiltepín
cascabel
Morita

Part Three: The Recipes

Basic recipes for salsas, sauces and condiments precede the main recipes, which start on page 44

SAUCES AND SALSAS

Chile Colorado (Basic Red Chile Sauce)

The chiles that are traditionally used for this sauce are the ones on *ristras* (strings of chiles). Stringing chiles is not just for decoration; it is a method of drying and preserving the chile crop for use throughout the year. Use this sauce in a number of dishes, as a topping for enchiladas and tacos, as a basis for stew—anything that calls for a red sauce. 🕐🕐

10 to 12 dried New Mexican red chiles
2 tablespoons vegetable oil
1 medium-size onion, chopped
2 garlic cloves, chopped
1 to 2 cups water or broth
1 teaspoon oregano, preferably Mexican
Pinch of ground cumin
Salt

Arrange the chile pods on a baking pan and place them in a 250°F oven for 10 to 15 minutes, or until the chiles become very aromatic. Be careful not to let them burn. Remove the stems and seeds and crumble the pods into a saucepan.

Cover the chiles with very hot water and allow them to steep for 15 to 20 minutes to soften. Drain them and remove from pan.

Sauté the onion and garlic in the oil until soft. Add the chiles and a couple of cups of water or broth and simmer for 10 minutes.

Place all the ingredients in a blender or food processor and puree them until smooth. Strain the mixture for a smoother sauce.

If the sauce is too thin, place it back on the stove and simmer until it is reduced to the desired consistency, or if too thick, add more water or broth. Adjust the seasonings and serve. Makes 2½ to 3 cups.

Time Estimates

Time estimates are for preparation only (excluding cooking) and are based on the assumption that a food processor or blender will be used.

🕐 *quick and very easy to prepare*

🕐🕐 *relatively easy; 15 to 30 minutes' preparation*

🕐🕐🕐 *takes more than 30 minutes to prepare*

Clockwise from top: Roasted Corn and Black Bean Salsa, Chile Piquín Salsa and Salsa Verde (recipes on pages 41–42).

Fresh Red Chile Sauce

In the fall, the last crop of chiles is allowed to remain on the plant to reach maturity and turn red. Once the chiles start to turn, their growing time is shortened as the plants begin to die back. The chiles at this stage develop a rich and complex flavor that produces a sauce with depth and layers—rather like the difference between a young wine and an aged one. Select pods that are full and plump, and prepare a lot of this sauce because it freezes well. ⌚

12 fresh New Mexican red chiles, roasted, peeled, stems and seeds removed
2 garlic cloves
½ teaspoon salt
½ teaspoon dried oregano, preferably Mexican
2 cups water

Place all the ingredients in a blender or food processor and puree until smooth, adding more water if necessary. Sometimes fresh chiles will still have fibers after they are pureed; strain if a smoother sauce is desired.

Adjust the seasonings to taste, heat the sauce over medium heat, and serve. Makes 2½ cups.

***Above**: Fresh Red Chile Sauce.*
***Right**: Green Chile Sauce.*
***Opposite page**: Chipotle Sauce.*

Green Chile Sauce

This is another classic sauce that is basic to the cuisine of Santa Fe. It is lightly flavored, with a pungency that ranges from medium to wild depending on the heat of the chiles. Adding finely diced pork or beef, omitting the tomatoes, and thickening with a roux of flour and oil are all popular variations. ⌚

2 tablespoons vegetable oil
1 small onion, chopped
1 garlic clove, minced
8 to 10 New Mexican green chiles, roasted, peeled and chopped (about 1 cup)
1 small tomato, peeled and chopped
2 to 3 cups chicken or vegetable broth
¼ teaspoon ground cumin
2 tablespoons cornstarch mixed with 3 tablespoons water

In a saucepan over medium heat, sauté the onion and garlic in the oil until soft.

Add the chiles, tomato, 2 cups of the broth and cumin. Bring the sauce to a boil, reduce the heat, and simmer for 10 minutes. Stir in the cornstarch mixture and continue to simmer for an additional 5 to 10 minutes to thicken. Add more broth to thin the mixture if the sauce becomes too thick.

Adjust the seasonings to taste, and serve. Makes 2 to 2½ cups.

Chipotle Sauce

Chipotles, smoked dried jalapeños, originated in the ancient civilization of Teotihuacán, near Mexico City, centuries before the Aztecs. The distinctive smoky and slightly sweet taste of these chiles adds layers of flavor to any sauce or dish. A word of caution: These chiles are hot and strong flavored; adding too many can overpower and overheat a dish, so start with a few and then add more until you reach the desired level of spiciness. ⌚⌚

ried New Mexican

eeled and chopped,
omatoes

3 tablespoons cider vinega
1 tablespoon brown sugar
1/2 teaspoon salt
1/4 teaspoon pepper
1/4 teaspoon ground cumin

Place the chiles in a large bowl and cover them with hot water. Steep until they're soft, 15 to 20 minutes. Drain the chiles and discard the water. Remove the stems and chop the chiles.

In a saucepan, sauté the onion in the oil until it's soft but not brown. Add the chiles and the remaining ingredients and simmer for 15 to 20 minutes to thicken.

Put the sauce in a blender or food processor and puree until smooth. Don't strain. Makes 3 cups.

Salsa Verde (Green Tomatillo Sauce)

Tomatillos, also called Mexican husk-tomatoes or *tomates verdes,* aren't tomatoes and don't even taste like them. They have a tangy, citruslike taste that can at times be very tart. This sauce can be used with and on other foods, or it can be served as a salsa with chips. ⌚

1 pound tomatillos, husks removed, chopped, or 1 (11-ounce) can of tomatillos, drained
½ cup diced white onion
2 garlic cloves, minced
2 or 3 *serrano* chiles (seeds included), minced
¼ cup chopped fresh cilantro
Sugar
Salt

If serving the sauce as a fresh salsa, combine all the ingredients in a bowl. Add sugar and salt to taste. Allow the salsa to sit for an hour before serving to allow the flavors to blend.

To serve the sauce hot, combine the tomatillos, onion, garlic and chiles in a pan. Simmer over low heat for a couple of minutes, until the tomatillos are soft but still colorful. Add sugar and salt to taste.

For a chunky sauce, stir in the cilantro and serve. Otherwise, put the sauce in a blender or food processor and puree until smooth. Add the cilantro and serve. Makes 2 to 2½ cups.

Chile Piquín Salsa

This salsa is served either smooth or with texture. It's best made with fully ripe tomatoes, but canned tomatoes may be substituted. In fact, the flavor is better with canned tomatoes than with underripe ones.
⌚

2 tablespoons crushed *piquín* chile, seeds included
1 cup hot water
6 plum tomatoes, chopped, or 2 cups canned tomatoes
1 (8-ounce) can tomato sauce
1 small onion, chopped
1 tablespoon red wine vinegar
1 teaspoon garlic powder
2 teaspoons sugar

Pinch of ground cumin
Pinch of oregano, preferably Mexican
Salt

In a mixing bowl, cover the chile with 1 cup of very hot water and steep for several minutes.

In a saucepan over medium heat, combine the remaining ingredients, the chile and the water in which the chile soaked and simmer for five minutes. If the salsa is too thick, thin it with water or broth to the desired consistency. Add salt to taste.

Allow the salsa to sit at room temperature for an hour to blend the flavors. Makes 2 cups.

Roasted Corn and Black Bean Salsa

Serve this colorful dish chilled as a salsa or warmed as a side dish or vegetable.

Right: Guacamole
Opposite page: New Mexican Green Chile Salsa (left) and Pico de Gallo (right).

2 ears fresh corn, or 1/2 cup canned or frozen whole-kernel corn, defrosted
1 medium-size tomato, chopped
1 small red onion, chopped
1/2 cup cooked black beans, rinsed and drained
1/4 cup chopped green or red bell pepper
2 jalapeño chiles, seeded and diced
1 garlic clove, minced
1 teaspoon oregano, preferably Mexican
1/4 teaspoon cumin seeds
3 tablespoons olive oil
2 tablespoons lime juice, fresh preferred
Salt

If using fresh corn, cut the kernels off the cobs using a sharp knife. Roast them over high heat in a dry, heavy skillet for a couple of minutes, or until the kernels are slightly browned, stirring constantly. Remove from heat.

Combine the corn, tomato, onion, beans, pepper, jalapeños, garlic, oregano and cumin, and gently mix. Whisk the oil and lime juice together, pour over the salsa and gently toss.

Allow the salsa to sit for an hour to blend the flavors before serving. Makes 2 1/2 to 3 cups.

New Mexican Green Chile Salsa

This salsa is best made with fresh New Mexican chiles, but canned chiles may be used.

4 to 5 New Mexican green chiles, roasted and peeled (1/2 cup chopped)
2 jalapeño chiles, diced (optional for added heat)
1 medium-size red onion, diced
3 garlic cloves, minced
2 tablespoons chopped fresh cilantro
1 teaspoon finely minced fresh oregano
1 (15-ounce) can diced tomatoes, drained (about 2 cups)
Salt

Combine all the ingredients in a bowl. Allow the salsa to sit for an hour at room temperature to blend the flavors before serving. Makes 2 1/2 to 3 cups.

Guacamole

This classic salsa goes well with any dish north or south of the border, and there are many variations. When buying avocados, look for those that are soft (or slightly soft) and then let them ripen. The quickest and easiest way to ripen them is to bury them in a container of flour for a day or two.

3 very ripe avocados, preferably Haas
1 small tomato, finely diced
1/4 cup minced white onion
2 *serrano* chiles, minced
1 small clove garlic, minced
2 teaspoons fresh lime or lemon juice
Salt

Cube the avocados and place them in a large bowl. Crush them with a fork or a masher until they're almost smooth but still retain a little texture. Mix in the remaining ingredients. Allow the guacamole to sit for an hour to blend the flavors before serving. Makes 1 to 1½ cups.

Helpful hint: To prevent the guacamole from turning black, squeeze a little lemon juice on the top. Cover with plastic wrap pressed into the surface so there are no air pockets. Another way is to put the avocado pit in the guacamole before covering it. Although there is some contention about whether this works, I always do it.

Pico de Gallo

Literally translated as "rooster beak," this salsa goes by a number of other names—*salsa fresca, salsa fria, salsa cruda* and *salsa Mexicana*. Whatever it's called, it is a wonderful salsa that you can serve with chips or as an accompaniment to a number of dishes. The secret to a good *pico de gallo* is in the texture. The ingredients should be finely chopped but not minced. ⌚

2 medium-size tomatoes, finely chopped
1 medium-size red onion, finely chopped
2 jalapeño chiles, finely chopped
2 garlic cloves, minced
1 bunch fresh cilantro, chopped (¼ cup)
3 tablespoons vegetable oil
3 tablespoons red wine vinegar
Salt

In a bowl, combine all the ingredients and mix thoroughly. Let the salsa sit at room temperature for at least an hour before serving. Makes 2 cups.

Helpful hint: The key to proper preparation is never to use a food processor or blender—all ingredients should be cut by hand to ensure a nice texture.

OTHER BASICS

Taco or Tostada Shells ⌚

Vegetable oil
12 corn tortillas

To prepare taco shells, pour oil in a heavy skillet to a depth of 1 inch and heat it until it's very hot. To test whether the oil is hot enough, dip in a small corner of the tortilla: if small bubbles rise, the oil is ready. Hold the tortilla with a pair of tongs and dip it into the oil for 5 to 10 seconds. Fold the tortilla in half and hold it open with the tongs while it cooks, to shape one side. When the tortilla is crisp, after about 20 seconds, turn it over and repeat the procedure with the other side. Remove the taco and drain it on paper towels. You need to hold the tacos open so there will be room for the fillings.

To make tostada shells, follow the same procedure, but make a small slit in the center of the tortilla and don't fold it. Makes 12 taco or tostada shells.

GOAT CHEESE AND ROAST PEPPER QUESADILLAS

Santa Fe School of Cooking

Quesadillas are stuffed flour tortilla turnovers that can be toasted, fried, or baked—a type of Southwestern or Mexican sandwich. These appetizers or snacks can be filled with just about any mixture, but cheese is the most common filling. In this recipe, the quesadillas are open rather than folded. 🕐🕐

8 (8-inch) flour tortillas
2 cups (½ pound) grated Monterey jack cheese
1 cup (¼ pound) crumbled goat cheese
3 tablespoons olive oil
1 medium-size onion, thinly sliced
2 garlic cloves, thinly sliced
1 red bell pepper, roasted and cut into thin strips
1 yellow bell pepper, roasted and cut into thin strips
1 or 2 *poblanos* or New Mexican green chiles, roasted, peeled, seeded and cut into thin strips
Salt and freshly ground black pepper
Fresh basil or oregano (optional)

Preheat the oven to 350°F. Place the tortillas on a flat surface and sprinkle each one with ¼ cup of jack cheese. Sprinkle 1 tablespoon of goat cheese over the jack.

Heat the oil in a large skillet over medium-high heat. Add the onion and sauté until it is translucent. Add the garlic and continue to cook until the garlic is lightly golden.

Add the red and yellow pepper strips, and the chile strips, combining them thoroughly. Season to taste.

Divide the sautéed ingredients among the tortillas and top with additional goat cheese.

Bake the quesadillas in the oven for 10 to 12 minutes, or until the cheese melts. Remove them from the oven and cut each quesadilla into 4 pieces and serve warm. Serves 4.

NACHOS

Corn Chips with Melted Cheese, Chiles and Pinto Beans

There are numerous variations of these popular appetizers. Nachos is another one of those dishes that you can vary to suit your tastes. Change the type of beans or cheese, add chorizo, change the chile, or even substitute crabmeat. There are no rules. ⏱

4 to 6 ounces tortilla chips, yellow, red, blue or a combination of all three
1/2 cup cooked pinto beans, drained
1/4 cup sliced pickled jalapeño chiles, drained
2 to 3 tablespoons sliced black olives
2 cups (8 ounces) grated cheddar cheese
Guacamole (optional) (page 42)
Sour cream (optional)
***Pico de Gallo* (optional) (page 43)**
Chopped fresh cilantro

Nachos served with guacamole (left) and sour cream is a classic Southwestern appetizer whose popularity has spread across the United States.

Preheat the oven to 400°F. Arrange the tortillas on a pan or ovenproof plate. Sprinkle the beans, chiles, olives and cheese over the chips and bake in the oven or under the broiler until the cheese melts.

Remove them from the oven, garnish with the cilantro, top with sour cream if so desired, and serve immediately with additional sauces on the side. Serves 4 to 6.

***Helpful hints**:* To prepare the nachos in a microwave, use a microwavable plate and microwave on high for 3 to 4 minutes.

To make homemade chips, cut corn tortillas into wedges and fry them in 400°F vegetable oil until crisp. Remove them from the oil and drain them on paper towels.

GRANDE

CATALAN PANCAKES WITH LOBSTER AND CRAB

Maurice Zeck, La Fonda

A Santa Fe version of pancakes from the Spanish region of Catalonia. ⌚⌚⌚

5 ounces small shrimp
5 ounces lobster meat
5 ounces Dungeness crab
1 tablespoon chopped shallots
$^1/_2$ cup white wine

Roasted Red Pepper Sauce

2 teaspoons clarified butter
1 tablespoon chopped shallots
8 ounces red bell peppers, roasted, peeled and pureed
$^1/_4$ cup seafood broth reserved from seafood for pancakes
2 tablespoons cornstarch mixed with 3 tablespoons water
Salt and ground white pepper to taste

The colorful Catalan Pancakes echo the vibrant painted windows of La Fonda's atrium dining room. They were painted by Ernesto Martinez, who has been a staff artist there for 48 years.

Pancakes

2 eggs
$^1/_2$ cup all-purpose flour
$^1/_4$ cup milk
Salt and ground white pepper
$^1/_4$ cup finely diced red pepper
5 tablespoons chopped fresh cilantro
2 scallions, sliced

Combine the seafood, shallots and wine in a sauté pan. Cover the pan and place over low heat until the seafood has released its juices and the shallots are soft but not browned. Strain off the liquid and reserve it.

To make the **roasted red pepper sauce**, heat the butter in a saucepan, add the shallots, and sauté until they are soft but not browned, 3 to 5 minutes. Add the pepper puree and broth and bring to a boil. Reduce the heat and simmer for 5 minutes. Slowly stir in just enough of the cornstarch mixture to thicken the sauce before serving. Add salt and white pepper to taste.

To make the **pancakes**, in a large bowl mix the eggs, flour, remaining seafood juice, milk, salt and pepper to form a batter. Stir in the red pepper, 3 tablespoons of the cilantro, the scallions and the seafood.

Heat a lightly oiled griddle until hot. Form silver-dollar-size pancakes and bake them on the griddle until they're cooked through, 3 to 4 minutes for each side, turning them only once. To serve, arrange 3 pancakes on a plate and top them with the sauce. Garnish the pancakes with the remainder of the cilantro and serve at once. Serves 4 to 6.

Helpful hint: To clarify butter, heat it in a saucepan or in a microwave oven, to separate the oil from the solids, and refrigerate. When it solidifies, discard the bottom sediment.

GRILLED SWORDFISH TACOS

Mark Kiffin, Coyote Cafe

These tacos are served with an unusual salsa. *Huitlacoche* is available frozen or in cans; either may be used in this recipe. Large scallions can be substituted for the Mexican bulb onions. ⌚⌚

Corn and Huitlacoche Salsa

1 tablespoon peanut or vegetable oil
½ cup minced white onion
4 *serrano* chiles, roasted, peeled, and chopped, seeds included
4 garlic cloves, roasted and mashed
2 cups (about 11 ounces) *huitlacoche*
5 plum tomatoes, diced
1 teaspoon minced fresh *epazote*
12 cilantro leaves
½ teaspoon salt
1 ear fresh corn, kernels cut off the cob
1 teaspoon *chipotle en adobo*

Cracked Coriander and Black Pepper Rub

¼ cup coriander seeds
2 tablespoons dried oregano
1 tablespoon black peppercorns
½ teaspoon sugar
¼ teaspoon salt

3 pounds swordfish, sliced into 1-pound pieces
1 pound Mexican bulb onions
18 (6-inch) white corn tortillas
1 bunch fresh cilantro
2 limes, sliced

To make the **salsa**, heat the oil in a sauté pan. Add the onion, *serrano* chiles and garlic and cook for 2 minutes to soften. Add the *huitlacoche,* tomatoes, *epazote,* cilantro and salt, and continue cooking for 15 minutes.

Soften the corn by placing it in a separate pan, adding 2 tablespoons of water, and cooking until the water has evaporated. Stir in the *chipotle en adobo,* and then add the corn to the *huitlacoche* mixture. Adjust the seasonings to taste.

Prepare the **rub** for the fish by placing all the ingredients in a dry skillet and toasting them over medium heat for 2 minutes, or until fragrant. Transfer the mixture to a spice grinder and grind until smooth.

Heat a grill. Rub the swordfish with the coriander and pepper mixture and grill the fish along with the bulb onions to desired doneness, about 8 minutes.

Soften the tortillas by dipping them in warm water and placing them on the grill or a hot pan. They will steam and soften.

To serve, slice the swordfish into 18 to 24 pieces allowing 3 to 4 pieces for each taco. Slice the onions and place them in the tacos along with the swordfish. Stack three tacos on a plate and garnish with cilantro sprigs and limes. Place the salsa on top or around the tacos and serve at once. Serves 6.

BLUE CRAB CAKES

Paul Hunsicker, Paul's Restaurant of Santa Fe

At Paul's, they serve these crab cakes with a delicious tomato-orange chipotle sauce.

1 pound (2 cups) cooked crabmeat, either fresh or canned, picked over for bits of shell
3 eggs, beaten
1 cup chopped fresh parsley
½ cup Dijon mustard
2 cups bread crumbs
¼ cup olive oil

Tomato-Orange Chipotle Sauce

2 cups chopped tomatoes
3 oranges, peeled, sectioned with membranes removed, finely chopped
1 red onion, finely chopped
¼ cup finely chopped fresh cilantro
3 *chipotles en adobo*, finely chopped
1 cup white wine
2 tablespoons butter
Salt and pepper
Red, yellow, and green bell pepper slices

In a large mixing bowl, combine the crabmeat, eggs, parsley, mustard and bread crumbs. Mix well and let stand a few minutes to blend the flavors.

To make the **tomato-orange chipotle sauce**, combine the tomatoes, oranges, onion, cilantro and chipotles in another bowl and set aside.

Form the crab mixture into 1½- to 2-ounce cakes. Heat the oil in a sauté pan over medium-high heat until very hot. Add the cakes, a few at a time, and fry them until they are well browned on both sides, turning only once. Remove them from the oil and drain them on paper towels.

To make the sauce, add the tomato mixture and wine to the pan in which the cakes were cooked. Bring to a boil, add the butter, and season with salt and pepper.

Arrange a couple of crab cakes on a plate, pour the sauce on top, garnish with bell pepper slices, and serve immediately. Serves 4.

TAPAS

Kit Baum, El Farol

Tapas, or hors d'oeuvres, are the "little bites" or small portions of dishes that are served with cocktails in the bars and taverns of Spain. Tapas can be eaten as an appetizer, or an assortment can be eaten as a meal.

Clockwise from top: Moroccan Eggplant with Cilantro Pesto, Sauteéd Wild Mushrooms with Spaghetti Squash, Tortilla Española, Ceviche and Gambas al Ajillo. The plates were produced in the shop of the Aguilar family, in Pueblo, Mexico, which has been crafting fine pottery for three generations.

GAMBAS AL AJILLO (Spicy Sautéed Shrimp) ⌚⌚

1/4 cup olive oil
4 whole garlic cloves plus 1 tablespoon minced garlic
3/4 pound medium-size shrimp, peeled and deveined
2 tablespoons fresh lime juice
2 tablespoons butter
1/2 teaspoon ground paprika
Pinch of crushed piquín chile
1/4 to 1/3 cup lamb or beef stock, lightly seasoned with a pinch of ground cloves, cinnamon and dried thyme
2 tablespoons dry Madeira
Salt and freshly ground black pepper
2 tablespoons coarsely chopped fresh Italian parsley

In a large sauté pan or a heavy-bottomed pan, heat the olive oil with the whole garlic cloves over the highest heat until smoking. Add the shrimp and quickly turn them over and cook for a few seconds to seal in the flavor. Remove the pan from the heat.

Pour out all of the oil and discard the garlic. Return the shrimp to the pan over medium-high heat.

Pour the lime juice over the shrimp and add the butter, minced garlic, paprika, *piquín,* lamb stock, and Madeira. Simmer until the shrimp has turned pink, a couple of minutes. Season with salt and pepper. Toss the shrimp with the parsley and serve immediately. Serves 4.

CEVICHE ⌚⌚

In ceviche, raw fish is "cooked" without heat, through a chemical reaction with an acid, such as lime juice. The flavors in this dish cleanse the palate.

1 pound bay scallops
1/2 pound small shrimp, peeled and deveined
1/2 pound small squid, body cut into rings, tentacles separated
2 bunches scallions, thinly sliced (1 cup)
1 bunch fresh cilantro, finely chopped (1/2 cup)
1 large jalapeño chile, chopped
2 to 3 cups fresh lime juice

Place all the ingredients except the lime juice in a nonreactive bowl. Pour the juice over the mixture to cover. Marinate in the refrigerator for 2 hours.

Serve the ceviche chilled. Makes 6 to 8 servings.

SAUTÉED WILD MUSHROOMS WITH SPAGHETTI SQUASH

1 spaghetti squash (about 2 pounds)
3 tablespoons unsalted butter
1 tablespoon olive oil
1 slice uncooked bacon, diced
6 to 8 ounces sliced wild
  mushrooms, such as oyster or portobello
1 scallion, sliced
2 tablespoons medium-sweet sherry
2 to 4 tablespoons lamb or beef stock
Salt and freshly ground black pepper
Chopped fresh Italian parsley

Preheat the oven to 450°F. Cut the squash in half lengthwise, scoop out the seeds, and rub the butter over the squash. Place on a baking pan lined with aluminum foil. Bake for 30 to 40 minutes, or until the squash is tender.

In a sauté pan over medium heat, add the oil and bacon and cook until all the fat has been rendered from the bacon. Add the mushrooms and scallion and toss until coated. Sauté until the scallion is tender and slightly browned, about 5 minutes.

Raise the heat, add the sherry and deglaze the pan. Reduce the heat, stir in the lamb stock, and heat through, a couple of minutes. Season to taste with salt and pepper.

To serve, pull the long strands out of the squash with a fork and place them on a serving plate. Spoon the mushrooms over the squash, garnish with the parsley, and serve at once. Serves 6 to 8.

MOROCCAN EGGPLANT WITH CILANTRO PESTO

1 large or 2 small eggplants
Vegetable oil

Cilantro Pesto

1 large bunch fresh cilantro, stems
  removed (about 2 cups)
$\frac{1}{4}$ cup lemon juice
$\frac{1}{2}$ cup olive oil
$\frac{1}{2}$ teaspoon ground cumin
Salt

1 red bell or pimiento pepper,
  roasted, peeled and thinly sliced
2 teaspoons coarsely chopped Italian parsley
4 to 6 tablespoons olive oil
Black olives

Preheat the oven to 375°F. Pierce the eggplant liberally with a fork and coat it with the oil. Place on a baking pan and bake for 25 minutes. Turn the eggplant over and continue to cook for an additional 20 minutes, or until it is only slightly firm. Remove it from the oven and allow to cool to room temperature.

To make the **pesto**, thoroughly clean the cilantro and chop it in a food processor. While it's processing, gradually add the remaining ingredients until the mixture is a deep green, aromatic puree.

When the eggplant has cooled enough to handle, remove the skin and try to remove most of the seeds with a fork. But don't sacrifice good eggplant meat to be seed-free. Coarsely chop the eggplant into bite-size chunks and place them neatly in a shallow earthenware or glass pan for serving.

Garnish with roasted red pepper, sprinkle on the parsley, and coat lightly with the olive oil. Serve accompanied with individual bowls of pesto and black olives. Makes 6 servings.

TORTILLA ESPAÑOLA
(Spanish Tortilla)

A traditional tapa, this Spanish omelet is made with potatoes and eggs and is served, at room temperature, with romesco sauce. ⌚⌚⌚

3 pounds (approximately 10 medium-size potatoes), peeled and sliced into 1/8-inch slices
1/3 cup olive oil
1 medium-size onion, thinly sliced
6 eggs, beaten
1/4 teaspoon salt

Romesco Sauce

3/4 cup toasted almonds
10 garlic cloves
1/2 cup olive oil
1/4 cup red wine vinegar
2 to 3 dried *piquín* chiles
2 cups red bell peppers, roasted, peeled and seeded
Salt

Preheat the oven to 350°F. In a small roasting pan, toss the potatoes with the oil, cover, and bake for 20 minutes. Uncover the pan and spread the onion slices evenly over the potatoes. Cover and bake for an additional 10 minutes, or until the potatoes are just done. Remove the pan and pour off the oil, reserving it. Cool the potatoes to room temperature.

Meanwhile, prepare the **romesco sauce**. In a blender or food processor, puree the almonds, garlic, oil, vinegar and chiles until smooth. Add the peppers, replace the top, and pulse until the sauce is just a bit chunky. Salt to taste.

Season the eggs with the salt. Gently fold the potato-and-onion mixture into the eggs and mix carefully.

Heat a nonstick sauté pan over high heat with a few tablespoons of the reserved oil. When it's hot, carefully add the egg mixture. Allow the eggs to set on a high heat for a minute while gently shaking the pan so they don't stick. Reduce the heat to the lowest temperature and cook for 15 to 20 minutes, or until the mixture is firm.

Place a plate on top (upside down as you look at it) of the sauté pan and flip the tortilla onto the plate. (Do this over your sink.) Reheat the skillet over high heat and carefully slide the tortilla back into the pan. Reduce the heat to low and cook the other side until it's done, about 8 minutes. When the tortilla feels firm to the touch, it's done.

Cool the tortilla to room temperature, slice it into wedges. When you are ready to serve the tortilla, spoon some of the romesco sauce onto a plate and place a wedge on top. Serves 6.

LOBSTER CEVICHE WITH PLANTAIN CHIPS

Mark Kiffin, Coyote Cafe

This is another version of ceviche that uses lobster meat instead of the traditional scallops, shrimp, and squid. It is important that only the freshest fish be used to make a quality ceviche. ⌚⌚

2 lobsters, cooked and shelled (1½ pounds each)
1 medium-size tomato, diced
1 medium-size red onion, diced
1 cucumber, peeled, seeded and diced
Juice of 2 limes
1 teaspoon commercial *habanero* sauce
½ teaspoon salt
1 teaspoon olive oil
2 avocados, diced
Fresh cilantro sprigs

Plantain Chips

2 green plantains, thinly sliced lengthwise
Vegetable oil
Salt
1 fresh lime, halved

Slice the lobster meat, toss with the tomato, onion, cucumber, lime juice, *habanero* sauce, salt and olive oil. Chill in the refrigerator for half an hour to an hour.

To make the chips, heat the oil to 300°F. Fry the plantains until they're crisp but not dark. Remove them from the oil, drain them, and season them with the salt and lime juice while they're still warm.

To assemble, toss the lobster mixture with the diced avocado or layer them in a tall sundae glass. Garnish with the cilantro sprigs and plantain chips and serve. Serves 6.

GARLIC SOUP

With its roots in both Spain and Mexico, this version of a classic soup uses bread as a thickener. The garlic should be cooked very slowly so that it is soft and "creamy," not browned. The amount of garlic may be adjusted to suit your tastes.

¼ cup olive oil
8 to 10 garlic cloves, finely sliced
2 slices French bread, crusts removed, cubed
1 quart chicken broth
1 sprig fresh *epazote*
Salt and freshly ground black pepper
4 eggs, beaten
Chopped cilantro or parsley
Lime wedges

Heat a heavy skillet over medium-low heat, add the oil and garlic, and cook gently until the garlic is golden, about 15 minutes. Remove the garlic from the oil and reserve. Return the pan to the heat and sauté the bread until golden.

Place the garlic and bread in a saucepan over medium heat. Add the broth and *epazote,* cover, and simmer until the bread breaks down and mixes with the broth, 10 to 15 minutes. Season to taste with the salt and pepper. Raise the heat and stir in the eggs until they are cooked.

Garnish the soup with the cilantro and serve it immediately with the lime wedges on the side. Serves 4.

BLACK BEAN SOUP

Rosalea Murphy, The Pink Adobe Restaurant

Turtle beans, or black beans, are native to South America. Their slightly mushroomlike flavor enhances dishes throughout South and Central America, the Caribbean and New Mexico. If you don't have time to soak the beans overnight, substituting canned beans also works well.

The rich colors and textures of Black Bean Soup (left) and Mexican Corn Chowder (recipe on page 132) are right at home on a table painted by Rosalea Murphy, owner of The Pink Adobe Restaurant.

1 cup (1/2 pound) dried black beans, soaked overnight
1/2 green bell pepper, or 4 to 5 fresh New Mexican green chiles, roasted, peeled and chopped (about 1/2 cup)
2 tablespoons olive oil
1 1/2 large onions, chopped
2 garlic cloves, minced
3/4 pound ham hock
4 cups beef broth
1 1/2 teaspoons ground cumin
1 1/2 teaspoons dried oregano
1/4 teaspoon dried thyme
1/2 bay leaf
1/4 cup chopped pickled jalapeño chiles
1 tablespoon dry sherry
Salt and freshly ground black pepper
Diced tomato
Chopped scallions
Sliced hard-cooked eggs
Sour cream

Wash the beans and place them in a stockpot along with the bell pepper. Add enough water to cover the beans, and soak them overnight. Drain the beans.

Heat the oil in a heavy skillet, add the onion and garlic, and sauté for 3 minutes over medium heat.

Combine the onion mixture, beans and ham hock in a large stockpot and cover them with the broth. Raise the heat to just below boiling, then reduce the heat and simmer for 1 hour.

Add the herbs, jalapeños and sherry, and season with the salt and pepper. Continue to cook for an additional 1 1/2 hours, or until the beans are done.

To thicken the soup, remove about 1/2 cup beans from the pot, mash them, and return them to the pot. Stir well and adjust the seasonings to taste.

To serve, ladle the soup into bowls. Garnish with the tomato, scallions, egg, and sour cream and serve immediately. Serves 4 to 5.

GREEN CHILE STEW

This dish has been a popular staple in Santa Fe for hundreds of years, ever since the Spanish introduced domesticated pigs. Although it's a simple dish, the slow simmering blends the flavor of the pork so well with the chile that sometimes I make it with just pork and green chile.

1½ pounds lean pork, cut into 1½-inch cubes
Vegetable oil
1 large onion, diced
2 garlic cloves, minced
1 quart pork or chicken broth
6 New Mexican green chiles, roasted, peeled and cut in thin strips (about ½ cup)
2 small tomatoes, peeled and chopped
1 large potato, peeled and diced
½ teaspoon dried oregano, preferably Mexican
Salt

In a heavy skillet, brown the pork over medium to medium-high heat, adding a little oil if needed. When the pork is browned, transfer it to a large stockpot. Add the onion and some more oil to the same skillet and sauté until the onions turn a golden brown, 5 to 10 minutes. Add the garlic and cook for an additional minute. Transfer the mixture to the pot with the pork.

Add 2 cups of pork broth to the skillet, raise the heat, and deglaze the skillet, being sure to scrape all the bits and pieces from the sides and bottom. Pour the broth over the pork in the stockpot.

Add the remaining ingredients to the stockpot, bring it to just below boiling, reduce the heat, and simmer for 1 to 1½ hours, or until the meat is very tender and starts to fall apart. Serves 4.

Helpful hint: For a meatless alternative, substitute pinto beans (which have been soaked overnight) and vegetable broth.

HUEVOS RANCHEROS

Breakfast Eggs with Corn Tortillas and Chile Sauce

Huevos Rancheros served with Blue Corn Chimayó Chile Bacon Muffins. The muffin recipe is on page 132.

The basic recipe for this dish calls for salsa, tortillas and eggs, but there are a number of variations. For instance, the eggs can be fried and placed on the sauce or poached right in the sauce; the salsa can be homemade or prepared—you can even try the Green Chile Sauce (page 40) instead of or along with the roasted red tomato sauce.

Roasted Red Tomato Sauce

1½ pounds plum tomatoes
2 New Mexican green chiles
2 garlic cloves, unpeeled
1 small white onion, diced
2 teaspoons vegetable oil
2 teaspoons cider vinegar
1 teaspoon sugar
¼ teaspoon ground cumin
¼ teaspoon dried oregano
1 tablespoon lime juice
Salt

Vegetable oil
4 corn tortillas, yellow or blue corn
4 eggs
Grated cheddar cheese

To make the **roasted red tomato sauce**, place the tomatoes, chiles and garlic in a baking pan under the broiler, or on a screen over a gas flame, and roast them until their skins blister and blacken, turning them frequently. Allow the vegetables to cool. Peel them and chop the tomatoes, seed and dice the chiles, and mince the garlic.

In a saucepan over medium heat, sauté the onion in the oil until it's soft and translucent, about 5 minutes. Add the roasted vegetables, vinegar, sugar, cumin and oregano and simmer for 3 to 4 minutes to release the tomato juices and thicken the sauce. Add the lime juice, season with the salt, and simmer for another couple of minutes.

Pour the oil in a skillet to a depth of 1 inch and heat it over a high flame. When the oil is very hot, make a small slit in the center of a tortilla so that it doesn't puff up, and fry it for a few seconds until it's crisp. Remove it from the oil, drain it, and repeat the procedure with the remaining tortillas. Pour off all but a teaspoon of the oil.

Break the eggs into the skillet and fry them to desired doneness.

To assemble the dish, place a tortilla on each plate and spoon on some of the sauce. Slip the eggs on top of the sauce, garnish with the cheese, and serve immediately. Serves 4.

***Helpful hint**:* Don't worry about removing all the blackened skins from the vegetables. A few pieces will add to the roasted flavor.

RADIO

CHILES RELLENOS

Stuffed Green New Mexican Chiles

Relleno means "stuffed," and we make these rellenos with cheese, a meat mixture, or a combination of meat, dried fruits, and nuts. They are best made with fresh New Mexican chiles, but canned ones may be substituted. See page 128 for illustrated instructions on preparing *chiles rellenos*. 🕐🕐

4 large, or 8 small, New Mexican green chiles, roasted, peeled and seeded, with stems on
$^1/_3$ to $^1/_2$ pound cheddar or Monterey jack cheese, cut into sticks
All-purpose flour
3 eggs
3 tablespoons flour
1 tablespoon water
$^1/_4$ teaspoon salt
Vegetable oil
1 recipe red or green chile sauce (chose from any of the recipes on pages 39–40)

Make a slit in the side of each chile and carefully stuff it with the cheese sticks. If the chiles tear, secure them with a toothpick. Just be sure to remove it before serving the chile.

Place some of the flour on a plate and roll each of the chiles in the flour until it's fairly evenly covered. Shake off the excess and set aside the chiles.

Separate the eggs, putting the whites in a large bowl and the yolks in a small one. Whisk the egg yolks with the 3 tablespoons of flour, water and salt until they're thick and creamy. Set them aside.

Whip the egg whites until they form soft peaks. Set them aside while heating the oil.

Pour the oil in a sauté pan to a depth of $1^1/_2$ to 2 inches, or until it looks like it would reach a little more than halfway up the side of each chile. Heat the oil until a little of the batter quickly browns when dropped in the oil, about 20 seconds.

Quickly and gently fold the yolks into the whites so that the mixture is an even color but the whites are not broken down. Dip the chiles in the batter, covering them completely and removing any excess.

Slide the chiles, one or two at a time, into the hot oil. As they are browning on one side, carefully spoon some of the hot oil over the top to assist in setting the batter. When they're browned, gently turn them over and brown the other side, turning only once. Remove them from the oil, drain them, and continue the procedure with the remaining chiles.

Place a couple of spoonfuls of the chile sauce on a plate, place the rellenos on top, and serve immediately. Serves 4.

Helpful hint: It is better to underwhip the egg whites than to overwhip them. If they are too firm, the whites may break down when the yolks are added. If they're softer, the batter will be thinner, and the coating not as thick, though the taste is just as good.

SOUTHWEST SUMMER VEGETABLE TAMALES

Southwest Summer Vegetable Tamales (left) and Venison Red Chile Stew (recipe on page 133).

The name *tamale* comes from the Nahuatl Indian word *tamalli,* and it is one of the oldest Mexican foods. Traditionally, lard has been used as the fat in making tamales, but for the health-conscious, vegetable shortening may be substituted. ⌚⌚⌚

Filling

2 cups whole-kernel corn, fresh or frozen
1 large zucchini, diced
1 small onion, diced
1/4 cup chopped New Mexican green or *poblano* chile, roasted, seeded and peeled
1 teaspoon chopped fresh marjoram, or 1/2 teaspoon dried
1 cup Green Tomatillo Sauce (page 41)
Salt and freshly ground black pepper
1 cup grated *asadero* or Monterey jack cheese

Tamales

24 dried corn husks
4 cups dried masa
1/2 teaspoon baking powder
1 teaspoon salt
2 1/2 cups vegetable broth or water
2/3 cup shortening

For the filling, combine the corn, zucchini, onion, chile and marjoram in a large bowl. Add the tomatillo sauce and lightly mix the ingredients. Season with salt and pepper and set the mixture aside.

Place the corn husks in a shallow pan, cover them with water, and soak them for 15 to 20 minutes to soften.

In another bowl, mix together the masa, baking powder and salt. Slowly add the broth until the mixture holds together.

Whip or beat the shortening until it's fluffy. Add the masa to the shortening and continue to beat the mixture until it's fluffy. Drop a teaspoonful of the dough into a glass of cold water: if it floats, it is ready. If it sinks, continue to beat it. Test until it floats.

To assemble, place a couple of tablespoons of the masa in the center of a large husk, or 2 smaller husks that overlap, and spread thinly. Place a couple of tablespoons of the filling down the center of the masa and sprinkle on a little of the cheese. Fold the husks over and tie (see page 129).

Place a rack in the bottom of a steamer or large pot and add water to cover the bottom. Arrange the tamales either standing up or in layers, but do not pack them tightly, because they expand as they cook. Cover the tamales with a towel or additional corn husks. Steam them until the masa has cooked, 30 to 40 minutes. To test for doneness, open the end of one tamale—if the masa pulls away from the wrapper, the tamales are done.

Allow them to cool slightly and serve with additional tomatillo sauce. Makes 24 tamales.

POBLANO RELLENO

Roasted Poblano Chiles Stuffed with Quinoa, Mushrooms and Pine Nuts

This is another chile relleno with a delicious mushroom, quinoa and goat cheese filling. Piñon trees grow extensively throughout northern New Mexico, and the nuts have been gathered and used in cooking for hundreds of years. The delicate yet nutty flavor of the quinoa (pronounced KEEN-wah) is enhanced by the addition of the nuts. See page 128 for information on stuffing a chile. ⌚⌚⌚

Filling

1 cup quinoa
1/4 cup sliced mushrooms, such as shiitake, portobello or crimini
2 shallots, sliced
1 garlic clove, minced
2 tablespoons butter or olive oil
1 teaspoon fresh thyme
1/2 teaspoon dried sage
1/8–1/4 teaspoon ground *chile de Árbol*
1 cup goat cheese
3 tablespoons New Mexican piñon nuts or regular pine nuts
Salt

4 *poblano* chiles, roasted, peeled and seeded, with stems left on
1 recipe Fresh Red Chile Sauce (page 40)

Preheat the oven to 350°F. To make the **filling**, begin by rinsing the quinoa twice in a fine strainer. Place it in a saucepan and cover it with water (the water should be 1 inch above the surface of the grain). Bring to a boil, reduce the heat, and simmer until all the liquid has been absorbed, 15 to 20 minutes. Transfer the quinoa to a mixing bowl and fluff with a fork.

In a small skillet over medium heat, sauté the mushrooms, shallots and garlic in the butter until they've softened, about 5 minutes. Add the thyme, sage and chile and sauté for an additional minute. Remove the skillet from the heat and add its contents, along with the cheese and pine nuts, to the quinoa. Combine well and salt to taste.

Stuff the chiles with the filling, place them on an oiled baking pan, and warm them in the oven.

Place a *poblano relleno* on each plate, top it with the chile sauce, and serve. Makes 4 servings.

STEAK DUNIGAN

Rosalea Murphy, The Pink Adobe Restaurant

This dish was named after its inventor, Pat Dunigan, who insisted on adding green chiles to his steak whenever he ate at the restaurant. Soon there was such a demand for a steak with chiles that Rosalea had to put it on the menu. It has become a signature dish of the Pink.

Green Chile Sauce

2 tablespoons olive oil
1 medium-size onion, finely chopped
2 (4-ounce) cans New Mexican green chiles, drained and chopped
1/4 teaspoon dried oregano
1/4 teaspoon salt
1 teaspoon Tabasco sauce or chopped jalapeño chile

4 large fresh mushrooms, thinly sliced
4 tablespoons butter (1/2 stick)
Hickory-smoked salt or regular salt
2 top-grade (14- to 15-ounce) New York sirloin steaks

To prepare the **green chile sauce**, heat the oil in a saucepan over medium-high heat and sauté the onion until it's soft and translucent, approximately 5 minutes. Add the remaining sauce ingredients, reduce the heat, and simmer for an additional 5 minutes. Keep the sauce warm in a 200°F oven.

In another pan over medium heat, sauté the mushrooms in the butter until they're soft, approximately 5 minutes. Remove the pan from the heat and also keep it warm in the oven.

Shake the hickory salt on both sides of the steaks. Broil or grill to the desired doneness (10 to 15 minutes for rare; 15 to 20 minutes for medium), turning them once.

Transfer the steaks to individual plates and divide the mushrooms over them. Cover each with the green chile sauce and serve at once. Serves 2.

CARNE ASADA

Grilled Steaks with Chimayó, Chile and Cumin

Carne asada means "grilled meat," and this dish is very similar to those *asadas* served in Mexico. Quick and easy to prepare, these steaks are usually served with a tomato-based salsa, such as Pico de Gallo, that complements the hearty beef flavor.

3 fresh limes
4 ribeye steaks
4 to 5 garlic cloves, chopped
1 tablespoon ground red *Chimayó* chile
1 teaspoon freshly ground black pepper
1 teaspoon ground cumin
$^1/_4$ cup olive oil
2 cups salsa, such as *Pico de Gallo* (page 43) or New Mexican Green Chile Salsa (page 42)
8 corn tortillas

Cut the limes in half and squeeze the juice over both sides of the steaks. Rub the garlic on the steaks; sprinkle the chile, pepper and cumin over the steaks; and marinate them for 30 minutes at room temperature.

Prepare a charcoal grill. When the coals are medium hot, brush the steaks with oil and grill them to the desired doneness.

Immediately serve the steaks, accompanied with the salsa and warm corn tortillas. Serves 4.

CARNE ADOVADA

Al Lucero, Maria's New Mexican Kitchen

This simple to prepare but very tasty dish evolved from the need to preserve meat without refrigeration. Since chile acts as an antioxidant, covering or marinating pork in a chile sauce kept the meat from spoiling before the advent of the icebox. One of the most popular dishes in New Mexico, *carne adovada* is on the menu for breakfast, lunch, and dinner. ⓓⓓⓓ

Carne Adovada with flour tortillas and Pico de Gallo served in a petroglyph-inspired platter. The word petroglyph comes from the Greek words meaning "rock" and "carving." In the Southwest they were made by several Native American cultures.

2 pounds pork butt

Red Chile Sauce

6 to 8 dried New Mexican red chile pods
4 garlic cloves
½ teaspoon salt
3 cups water

1 cup crushed New Mexican red chile, seeds included
1 tablespoon garlic powder
1 teaspoon salt
6 flour tortillas
1 recipe *Pico de Gallo* (page 43)

Preheat the oven to 375°F. Trim the fat from the pork and cut the meat into 1-inch cubes. Put the meat in a lightly oiled or sprayed deep baking pan and bake it for 30 minutes, stirring often to ensure even cooking.

To make the **red chile sauce**, place the chiles in a medium-size saucepan and cover them with hot water. Steep until they're soft, about 20 minutes. Drain them and discard the water.

Place the chile pods, garlic, salt, and water into a blender or food processor and puree the mixture until it's smooth, adding additional water if necessary. Pour the mixture into the saucepan and simmer until it thickens slightly.

Remove the baking pan from the oven but do not pour off the juices. Stir in the red chile sauce, the crushed chile, garlic powder and salt. Return it to the oven and bake, stirring occasionally, until the pork is tender enough to cut with a fork, 30 to 45 minutes.

Serve the *carne adovada* with the flour tortillas, accompanied by the *Pico de Gallo.* Serves 6.

RACK OF LAMB WITH HEIRLOOM BEAN RAGOUT

Jeff Copeland, Santacafé

The lamb for this dish should be "frenched", that is, the meat should be cut away to expose the end of the bone, as in the photo. It's easiest to have a butcher do this. This dish uses three heirloom beans, but any three-bean combination will taste good. Try substituting black-eyed peas, white northern or even pinto beans; you can also use canned beans to reduce the cooking time. Pomegranate molasses, which can be found in most import or Indian markets, makes a nice glaze for the lamb.

1/4 cup dried Anasazi beans
1/4 cup dried palomino beans
1/4 cup dried rattlesnake beans
5 tablespoons unsalted butter
1 medium-size yellow onion, julienned
1 medium-size red onion, julienned
1 tablespoon chopped garlic
2 cups veal demiglace or chicken stock
4 (12-ounce) frenched racks of lamb
Salt and freshly ground black pepper
Olive oil
1 cup pomegranate molasses
1 cup (2 ounces) lightly chopped fresh herbs such as thyme, rosemary, sage or marjoram

Place each of the beans in separate bowls, cover them with water, and refrigerate them overnight.

In separate saucepans, cook the beans until they're tender, 1 to 2 hours. It is important to keep them separate because they have different cooking times. Drain the beans and keep them warm.

Preheat a grill or oven to 400°F, or a broiler, depending on how you want to cook the lamb. If you choose to use an oven, be sure to also preheat the pan you will use to cook your lamb.

Heat 2 tablespoons of the butter in a large skillet or sauté pan over medium heat. When the butter starts to bubble, add the onion and sauté until it's caramelized, or brown. Add the garlic and beans and toss them in the skillet. Add the demiglace and simmer to reduce the sauce until it coats the back of a spoon.

Generously season the lamb with salt, pepper and a touch of the oil. Place it on the preheated cooking surface and cook to an internal temperature of 122°F. Remove and allow the meat to rest at room temperature, but no longer than 8 minutes.

Coat the lamb with the molasses, allowing a crust to form.

Stir the remaining butter into the bean mixture to thicken the sauce, and season with the fresh herbs, salt, and pepper.

Pile the beans in the center of a plate. Cut the lamb into chops and place them decoratively around the beans and serve immediately. Serves 4.

ORANGE-MARINATED CHICKEN FAJITAS

Santa Fe School of Cooking

Fajitas means "little belts"; traditionally they have been made with marinated and grilled skirt steak. Mexican-American cowboys are credited with creating the dish as a way of using tough, inexpensive cuts of meat. At the Santa Fe School of Cooking they serve Santa Fe Coleslaw and Pickled Red Onions as accompaniments. Note that this recipe requires advance preparation. ⌚

Clockwise from top: Orange-Marinated Chicken and Spanish Rice (page 104), flour tortillas, Pickled Red Onions (page 134) and Pico de Gallo (page 43), and Santa Fe Coleslaw (page 133).

Orange Marinade

3 large seedless oranges, unpeeled, cut into eighths
1 medium-size onion, cut into eighths
$^1/_2$ of a 7-ounce can of *chipotle en adobo* sauce
3 garlic cloves, peeled
$^1/_3$ cup coarsely chopped fresh cilantro
4 sprigs fresh rosemary, leaves only, or 2 teaspoons dried
4 sprigs fresh thyme, leaves only, or 1 teaspoon dried
4 sprigs fresh marjoram or oregano, leaves only, or 2 teaspoons dried
1 teaspoon kosher salt plus additional as needed

6 (4-ounce) skinless, boneless chicken breasts, trimmed of all fat and pounded to a thickness of $^1/_2$ inch
Salt
Vegetable cooking spray or vegetable oil
6 flour tortillas
1 recipe Santa Fe Coleslaw (page 133)
1 recipe Pickled Red Onions (page 134)

To make the **orange marinade**, combine the oranges, onion, *chipotles,* garlic, cilantro, herbs and salt in a food processor. Pulse until all the ingredients are thoroughly combined and the result is a rather coarse puree.

Place the chicken breasts in a plastic bag or layer in a nonreactive dish and spread the marinade over them. Marinate the chicken in the refrigerator for 12 to 24 hours. Clean the marinade from the chicken and season it with salt.

Coat a cast-iron grill pan with the cooking spray or oil it using a paper towel and heat over high heat until a drop of water sizzles upon contact, about 3 minutes. Reduce the heat to medium-high, and cook the chicken breasts until they're browned on one side, 3 to 5 minutes. Rotate the chicken 45 degrees about halfway through cooking to create crisscross grill marks. Turn over the breasts and cook until they are browned on both sides and done throughout but still juicy, 4 to 5 minutes.

Slice the chicken breasts into strips and serve with the flour tortillas, Santa Fe Coleslaw and Pickled Red Onions. Serves 6.

RED CORN RUBBED CHICKEN

Flynt Payne, Inn of the Anasazi

At the Inn of the Anasazi they serve this chicken with a tangy apple poblano slaw. ⌚⌚⌚

Habanero-Lime Molasses

1 cup molasses
Juice and zest of 1 lime
1 *habanero* chile, minced

2 red corn tortillas
5 *ancho* chiles
15 fresh cilantro leaves
1 egg, beaten
2 tablespoons all-purpose flour
Salt and freshly ground black pepper
2 chicken breasts, bone attached
2 tablespoons vegetable oil

The feet on this quirky stool, by artist James Holmes, are made out of buffalo horns.

Apple Poblano Slaw

1 Granny Smith apple, finely julienned
½ jicama, finely julienned
1 red bell pepper, finely julienned
1 *poblano* chile, finely julienned
Juice and zest of 1 lime
Zest of 1 lemon
1 tablespoon olive oil
1 tablespoon gold tequila
1 teaspoon brown sugar
Kosher salt and freshly ground black pepper
4 fresh mint leaves

To make the **habanero-lime molasses,** combine all the ingredients in a large saucepan. Bring the mixture to a simmer and cook it over low heat for 15 minutes, stirring often to prevent burning. Allow it to cool and strain it.

Preheat the oven to 350°F. Cut the tortillas into long, thin strips and place them in a bowl. Cut the *ancho* chiles into strips and add to the tortillas along with the cilantro leaves. Place the egg in a separate bowl. Season the flour with salt and pepper and place it in another bowl.

Dredge the chicken with the flour and dip it in the egg, then in the tortilla mix. Coat the chicken well and set it aside.

For the **apple poblano slaw** combine the apple, jicama, bell pepper and *poblano* chile in a large bowl. Add the lime juice and zest as well as the lemon zest, and toss. Combine the oil, tequila and sugar in a separate bowl and mix them well. Add this to the slaw, tossing to combine. Season with salt and pepper. Mix well and garnish with the mint leaves.

Heat the oil in a sauté pan over medium heat. Sauté the chicken in the pan until the tortilla pieces are lightly browned, then remove the chicken. Finish the chicken in the oven for 15 minutes, or until the juices run clear when the meat is pricked.

Place the chicken on individual plates and top each with the slaw. Drizzle the habanero-lime molasses over the entire plate. Serves 2.

TACOS AND TOSTADAS

A taco is a stuffed corn tortilla, which can be served either soft or crisp; a tostada is the flat version of a crisp taco. As with many tortilla-based dishes, the fillings are used interchangeably, and the types of fillings are limited only by your imagination.

Chicken and Beef Tacos (left) and Bean Tostadas.

Beef Filling

2 pounds beef chuck roast, cut into small pieces
2 cups beef broth or enough to cover the beef
2 *pasilla* chiles, stems removed, torn into pieces
1 dried New Mexican red chile, stem and seeds removed, torn into pieces
1 small onion, coarsely chopped
2 garlic cloves, chopped
1 teaspoon dried oregano, preferably Mexican
1/4 teaspoon ground cumin
Salt

Refried Beans

1 tablespoon vegetable oil
2 cups cooked pinto beans
1 cup bean liquid or water
1 tablespoon ground New Mexican red chile
1/4 teaspoon minced garlic
Pinch ground cumin
Salt

Chicken Filling

2 cups Chicken Enchilada Filling (page 90)

12 taco or tostada shells (page 43)
3 to 4 romaine lettuce leaves, finely shredded
1 large tomato, finely diced
1 cup (4 ounces) grated Monterey jack cheese
1 cup (4 ounces) grated cheddar cheese
1 recipe Chile *Piquín* Salsa (page 41) or New Mexican Green Chile Salsa (page 42)
Guacamole (page 42) (optional)
Sour cream (optional)

For the **beef filling**, cover the beef with water or broth in a large pot and add the *pasilla* chiles, onion, and garlic. Bring it to a boil, reduce the heat, cover and simmer until the meat is tender and starts to fall apart, about 1 hour. Allow the meat to cool in the broth until it's cool enough to handle. Remove and discard any fatty pieces, and using two forks or your fingers, shred the meat. Season the beef with the oregano, cumin, and salt.

To prepare the **refried bean filling**, heat the vegetable oil in a skillet over medium heat. Add the beans and the liquid and mash the beans to the desired consistency; they may all be smooth, or some beans may be left whole. Reduce the heat, stir in the chile, garlic and cumin, and simmer for 10 minutes, adding additional liquid if needed. Salt to taste.

To assemble, place the filling on the bottom of either a taco or a tostada shell, and then layer the remaining ingredients—lettuce, tomato and cheese—over the filling. Spoon guacamole and sour cream on top of the tacos or tostadas if desired. Serve with the salsa on the side. Makes 12 tacos or tostadas.

POLLO PIBIL

Katharine Kagel, Cafe Pasqual's

This spiced chicken dish came to Santa Fe by way of the Yucatán. The *pibil* method of cooking involves wrapping the meat in banana leaves, burying it in a pit, and roasting it slowly. The *achiote,* a paste of dried annatto seeds, is a sweet, earthy counterpoint to the citrus and garlic flavors. Be sure to allow plenty of time for marinating the chicken well; 24 hours is best. At Cafe Pasqual's they serve this dish with saffron rice and grilled vegetables.

Pollo Pibil with Saffron Rice (page 135) and Fire-Roasted Vegetables (page 134).

4 teaspoons cumin seeds
1 cinnamon stick, 3 inches long, preferably Mexican
1 teaspoon whole cloves
1½ tablespoons whole black peppercorns
½ cup *achiote* paste
3 tablespoons kosher salt
2 tablespoons finely minced garlic
2 cups orange juice, preferably fresh
½ cup lime juice, preferably fresh
2 tablespoons fresh marjoram leaves, or 1 tablespoon dried
½ cup olive oil
6 skinless, boneless chicken breasts, halved
Banana leaves
6 grilled scallions

To prepare the chicken, roast the cumin, cinnamon, cloves and peppercorns in a small, dry sauté pan over medium heat, shaking the pan frequently, until fragrant, about 2 minutes. Remove the spices from the heat and let them cool. Place the spices in a spice mill, coffee grinder or mortar and grind them until they're pulverized.

Put the spices, *achiote,* salt, garlic, orange and lime juices, marjoram and oil in a blender or food processor and process just long enough to blend.

Place the chicken breasts in a shallow nonreactive dish and pour the spice mixture evenly over the top to cover them completely. Cover the dish and let the chicken marinate in the refrigerator for at least 24 hours (up to 36 hours), turning it frequently.

Prepare a fire in a charcoal grill. When the coals are medium-hot, remove the chicken breasts from the marinade and place them skin-side down on the grill about 6 inches above the coals. Grill them, turning once, until they're done, 15 to 20 minutes' total grilling time. Be careful not to overcook them; the chicken should be juicy.

Garnish each breast with one grilled scallion and serve on a banana leaf. Serves 6.

BLUE CORN STACKED CHICKEN ENCHILADAS

The name *enchilada* refers to a dish of rolled or flat tortillas, usually corn, stuffed with a filling and topped with a chile sauce. These enchiladas can be either served whole as a main dish or cut into wedges and served as a side dish. ⌚⌚

Chicken Enchilada Filling

2 boneless chicken breasts, skin removed
2 tablespoons vegetable oil
1 medium-size onion, chopped
2 garlic cloves, minced
1 jalapeño chile, chopped
½ teaspoon ground cumin
½ teaspoon dried oregano, preferably Mexican
2 cups water or chicken broth

Blue Corn Stacked Chicken Enchiladas (left) and Chipotle Beef and Bean Burritos (right, page 131).

Enchiladas

Vegetable oil
12 blue corn tortillas
1 recipe either Basic Red Chile Sauce (recipe 39) or Green Chile Sauce (recipe 40)
2 cups shredded Monterey jack cheese
1 small onion, thinly sliced
¼ cup chopped fresh cilantro
Shredded lettuce
Chopped tomatoes

To prepare the **chicken enchilada filling**, cut it into large pieces. Heat the oil in a heavy skillet over medium-high heat, add the chicken, onion and garlic and sauté until the onion is soft, 5 to 10 minutes. Add the jalapeño, cumin, oregano and broth; cover the skillet; and simmer until the chicken is very tender and starts to fall apart, about 30 minutes. Remove the chicken from the heat and allow it to cool in the broth for 10 minutes. Remove the chicken. Using a couple of forks or your fingers, shred the chicken.

To make the **enchiladas**, preheat the oven to 300°F. Pour the oil in a skillet to a depth of 1 inch and heat it over a high flame until it's very hot. Make a small slit in the center of each tortilla to prevent it from puffing up and fry it for a couple of seconds on each side to soften, being careful it doesn't become too crisp. Remove the tortilla and drain it on paper towels.

To assemble the enchiladas, pour a small amount of the sauce of your choice on the bottom of a casserole dish, place a tortilla on top, then the chicken, some cheese, onion, cilantro and then more sauce. Repeat the procedure for an additional layer and finish with a tortilla. Spread additional sauce over the top. Repeat with the remainder of the tortillas and filling.

Place the enchiladas in an oven for 5 to 10 minutes, or until they're thoroughly heated.

To serve, pour additional sauce over the top and garnish with the lettuce, tomatoes and more shredded cheese. Serves 4.

CHILEAN SEA BASS NAPOLEON

Kelly Rogers, La Casa Sena

Chilean Sea Bass Napoleon served in the garden at La Casa Sena.

Kelly Rogers serves this layered dish over stir-fried chayote squash. ⌚⌚⌚

Tangerine Hot and Sour Sauce

1 teaspoon vegetable oil
1 jalapeño chile, chopped
1 tablespoon chopped fresh ginger
$2\frac{1}{2}$ teaspoons chopped garlic
2 cups tangerine juice
$\frac{1}{2}$ cup sugar
$\frac{1}{2}$ cup white wine
$\frac{1}{2}$ teaspoon salt
1 tablespoon cornstarch mixed with 3 tablespoons water

Charred Tomatillo Aïoli

6 tomatillos, husks removed
4 garlic cloves
2 slices red onion
Olive oil
Salt and freshly ground black pepper
Juice of 1 lime
1 cup mayonnaise

1 cup shelled pistachios
8 (2-ounce) pieces of Chilean sea bass
Olive oil
Salt and freshly ground black pepper

Fried tortilla triangles
Assorted greens (arugula, mâche, or romaine)
Tangerine zest

To make the **tangerine sauce**, heat the oil in a saucepan and sauté the jalapeño, ginger and garlic until lightly browned. Add the tangerine juice, sugar, wine and salt, and simmer to reduce the sauce by half. Remove the pan from the heat, strain the sauce, and return it to the stove. Simmer the sauce and slowly add the cornstarch mixture to thicken it.

For the **tomatillo aïoli**, lightly toss the tomatillos, garlic and onion in oil with a pinch of salt and pepper in a bowl. Grill the vegetables, or roast them in an oven, until they are blackened. Allow them to cool and place them in a blender or food processor with the lime juice and puree until smooth. Fold in the mayonnaise.

Preheat the oven to 250°F. Roast the pistachios in the oven until they're lightly browned, about 10 minutes. Let them cool, then chop the pistachios until fine in a food mill or with a knife.

Brush the fish with the oil, season with salt and pepper, and roll in the crushed pistachios. Grill the fish over medium-high heat for about 2 minutes total, turning the fish often so that the pistachios do not burn. The fish should be firm when done.

Build the Napoleon on each of 4 plates by alternating a fried tortilla triangle, aïoli, greens and fish. Repeat this procedure again, and top the fish and the plate with the tangerine sauce. Garnish with tangerine zest and serve immediately. Serves 4.

TROUT IN ADOBE

Kelly Rogers, La Casa Sena

Once you have cracked open the Trout in Adobe the trout tamale inside (opposite, right) is revealed.

The "adobe" in this recipe is a low-fire clay that can be found in an art or ceramics supply store. The trick to serving this dish is to take two large spoons and gently tap the baked clay to crack and break it, rather like using drumsticks, not like using an ax to split wood. It is **very important** to be certain that the clay you are using is non-toxic; many clays contain lead, which could contaminate the food. ⌚⌚⌚

8 to 12 corn husks
½ pound butter (2 sticks), softened
2 cups sliced mushrooms
1 tablespoon garlic, minced
½ cup white wine
Salt
5 pounds of potter's clay, divided into 1¼-pound slabs
4 whole trout, filleted, with skin and head removed (8 pieces)
Assorted greens (arugula, romaine, or mixed baby greens)
Lemon wedges

Preheat the oven to 400°F.

Place the corn husks in a shallow pan and cover them with water to soften.

Melt a couple of tablespoons of the butter in a sauté pan, add the mushrooms and garlic, and sauté until they're soft. Raise the heat, add the wine, season with the salt, and let the mixture cool slightly. Fold in the remaining butter and let the sauce cool until it's firm and malleable.

Using a rolling pin, roll out the clay until it is about 12 inches by 18 inches and ½ inch thick. Place ¼ of the firm butter mixture between 2 of the trout fillets. Repeat this step with the other 6 fillets.

Wrap each fish in 2 or 3 corn husks so that the fish is completely covered.

With the clay in front of you lengthwise, place the "tamale" on one side and fold over the clay. Cut out a fish shape and seal the clay with a fork around all edges. Cut vents in the sides to let air escape during cooking.

Place the fish either on a baking sheet or directly on the oven rack and bake for 15 to 20 minutes. The clay will get pale, dry and hard when it's done.

To serve, crack the clay with a large metal spoon and carefully push the clay off the "tamale." Take the "tamale" out and unfold the husks to expose the baked fish. Place it on a bed of prepared greens and garnish with lemons. Serves 4.

RAMP TART

Jeff Copeland, Santacafé

Ramps are wild onions that grow in deciduous forests in the spring. They have a long green shaft that is leafy at the top and crimson near the bulb. If picked while young, the whole plant is edible; otherwise only the bulb can be used. Most specialty food stores have ramps in the spring; but if they're not available, substitute scallions. ⌚⌚⌚

Ramp tart garnished with a fresh ramp at the Santacafé. The table's unusual legs are inspired by the petroglyph image of Kokopelli, the famous hunch-backed flutist.

Tart Shell

3 1/2 cups all-purpose flour
Pinch of salt
1 1/4 cups unsalted butter
3 egg yolks
1/4 cup ice water

2 teaspoons vegetable oil
1 medium-size red onion, julienned
1 teaspoon balsamic vinegar
1 1/2 pounds ramps or scallions
1 cup (11 to 12) egg yolks
1 1/2 cups heavy cream
Pinch of ground nutmeg
1/4 pound grated mild cheese, such as Monterey jack, *queso fresco,* farmer or goat cheese
Salt and freshly ground black pepper

To make the **tart shell**, combine the flour and salt in the bowl of an electric mixer. Add the butter and, using the whisk attachment, combine the mixture on a slow speed. When small chunks the size of rice form, add the yolks and increase the speed. Strain in the ice water and mix until combined. Allow the dough to rest in plastic wrap overnight or freeze it for later use. Bring the dough to room temperature before using.

Preheat the oven to 350°F. Roll out the dough on a lightly floured surface to a thickness of 1/8 inch and place it in an 8-inch tart or pie pan. Cover the pie dough with foil and fill the pan with dried beans or rice to keep the dough from bubbling. Bake for 12 minutes, or until the crust is golden brown and the center is cooked. Carefully take off the foil and weights. Let the crust cool at room temperature.

To make the filling, heat the oil in a sauté pan, add the onions and vinegar, and sauté over medium heat until the onions are browned. Remove the onions and set aside. Add the ramps to the pan with a little more oil and salt to keep them green. Cook until they're tender then set aside to cool.

Raise the oven temperature to 375°F. In a mixing bowl, combine the ramps and onions. In another bowl, whisk the egg yolks, cream and nutmeg.

To assemble, sprinkle the cheese on the bottom of the tart shell and add the onion mixture. Pour in the egg mixture, making sure not to fill the shell completely. Season with salt and pepper.

Cover the tart with foil and bake until the eggs are firm, 35 to 40 minutes. Remove the foil during the last 2 minutes so that the tart will lightly brown.

Allow the tart to cool slightly before serving. Serves 6 to 8.

CHIPOTLE CREMA MOREL STEW

Katharine Kagel, Cafe Pasqual's

The baked acorn squash makes an elegant serving dish for this tasty stew. 🕐🕐🕐

4 acorn squash, tops cut off but stems kept attached, seeds and strings removed and reserved for the stock

Vegetable Stock

2 tablespoons olive oil
2 garlic cloves, coarsely chopped
Celery leaves from ½ bunch of celery, roughly chopped
Potato peelings from 3 to 4 small red potatoes
2 small onions, unpeeled and quartered
Reserved seeds and strings from squash
1½ cups water

These eighteenth-century vice regal silver pieces from Peru are reminders of imperial Spain's influence in Santa Fe.

Stew

½ cup olive oil
½ cup carrots, cut into ½-inch dice
½ cup rutabaga, cut into ½-inch dice
¼ cup celery rib, cut into ½-inch slices
¾ cup zucchini or any summer squash, cut into 1-inch dice
3 to 4 small red potatoes (about ⅓ pound), cut into ½-inch dice
1 portobello mushroom, gills removed, thinly sliced
¼ cup fresh or rehydrated dried morels, quartered
1 garlic clove, finely minced
1 teaspoon grated fresh ginger
1½ cups heavy cream
2 teaspoons *chipotle en adobo*, pureed and strained

Preheat the oven to 300°F. Place the squash on a baking sheet, fill them with water, and place their tops back on. Cook them for 1 hour, or until they're fork-tender.

In a stockpot, sauté all the **vegetable stock** ingredients in oil over medium heat until they're lightly browned. Add 2½ cups of water and bring the mixture to a rolling boil. Skim off and discard any foam that forms. Reduce the heat and simmer the stock uncovered for 1 hour. Strain the stock, discard the vegetables, and reserve the stock.

In a large saucepan over medium heat, sauté all the **stew** ingredients except the cream and *chipotle* for 10 minutes. Add the reserved stock and simmer for 10 more minutes, or until the vegetables are fork-tender.

In another saucepan, simmer the cream until it's reduced by one-half.

Add the *chipotle* to the cream and stir until they're combined. Pour the mixture over the vegetables and gently mix in until well incorporated.

To serve, fill the baked squash with the stew, place the tops back on. Present the squash with garlic toast or other toasted bread. Makes 4 servings.

QUELITES & BEANS BORRACHO

Greens with Beans and Chile & Drunken Beans

QUELITES

The word *quelite* is derived from the Nahuatl word *quilitl,* which the Indians in ancient Mexico used to describe any edible leafy green or herb.

1½ pounds fresh spinach
½ small white onion, sliced and separated into rings
1 tablespoon vegetable oil
2 garlic cloves (optional)
½ cup cooked pinto beans
1 tablespoon crushed New Mexican red chile, seeds included
1 teaspoon distilled vinegar
Salt

Quelites (left) and Beans Borracho.

Rinse the spinach in a lot of water two or three times to remove any grit. Drain off the excess water and tear the leaves into smaller pieces, if necessary, and place them in a bowl.

In a sauté pan over medium-high heat, quickly sauté the onions in the oil until they soften, 1 or 2 minutes.

Prepare a steamer and place the garlic, if desired, in the water at the bottom. Toss the spinach with a little oil, and steam it until it's just soft, about 2 minutes.

Toss the spinach with the onions, beans, chile and vinegar. Season to taste with the salt and serve immediately. Serves 4.

BEANS BORRACHO

Borracho (which means "drunk") refers to the beer used to flavor the beans. Cooking the beans with garlic or *epazote* is said to help in digesting the beans. A little tequila can be substituted for the beer.

1½ cups dried bolita or pinto beans
2 garlic cloves
3 to 4 fresh *epazote* leaves, or 1 teaspoon dried
2 slices bacon, chopped (optional)
1 large onion, cut in thin wedges
1 (12 ounce) can of beer
2 small tomatoes, peeled and chopped
2 jalapeño chiles, cut into thin slices
Salt

Cover the beans with water and discard any that float to the surface. Soak the beans overnight.

Drain and rinse the beans. In a large pot, add the beans, water to cover, the garlic and the *epazote.* Bring the mixture to a boil, reduce the heat to medium-low, and simmer for 2 hours, or until the beans are tender. Add more water if needed. In a small skillet, fry the bacon until it's just crisp. Remove the bacon and drain it. Add the onion to the pan and sauté until it's soft, 3 to 5 minutes.

Drain off some of the bean water if the mixture is too soupy. Add all the remaining ingredients, adjust the seasonings to taste, and simmer for 20 to 30 minutes. Serves 4 to 6.

PAPAS CON CHILE COLORADO & CALABACITAS

Potatoes with Red Chile & Squash and Corn with Green Chile

PAPAS CON CHILE COLORADO

The word *colorado* in the title refers to the red color of the chile. These potatoes are commonly served in place of hash browns at breakfast as well as at lunch and dinner. They are especially tasty when made with new potatoes because of their creamy texture and taste. Substitute chopped New Mexican green chile for a totally different taste.

½ cup chopped onion
2 garlic cloves, minced
2 tablespoons vegetable oil
2 tablespoons crushed New Mexican red chile, seeds included
2 large potatoes, peeled and diced

Papas con Chile Colorado (left) and Calabacitas.

Preheat the oven to 350°F.

In a medium-size skillet over medium heat, sauté the onion and garlic in the oil until they soften and start to brown. Remove them from the heat and add the chile.

Toss the potatoes with the onion mixture until they're well coated and place them in a baking pan. Bake the potatoes for 40 minutes, or until they are tender. Serves 4.

CALABACITAS

For hundreds of years squash and corn have been the staples of the Pueblo Indians in northern New Mexico, and these vegetables are combined with chile in this popular dish. The delicate flavors of the corn and squash in combination with the bite of the chile acts as a basis for variations. Use different types of summer squash, add cheese (such as cheddar, Monterey jack, or feta), or include chicken to turn this recipe from a side dish into an entrée.

2 tablespoons vegetable or olive oil
2 zucchini squash, sliced
½ small white onion, sliced and separated into rings
2 cups whole-kernel corn, fresh, frozen or canned
½ cup (about 4 to 5) chopped New Mexican green chiles, roasted, peeled and seeded
2 teaspoons dried oregano
¼ to ½ cup heavy cream
Salt

In a sauté pan heat the oil over medium heat and sauté the squash and onion for a couple of minutes. The squash should be tender but not soft.

Add the corn, chile and oregano to the pan and sauté for 2 minutes. Stir in the cream, add salt to taste, and simmer for 3 to 4 minutes to blend the flavors. Serves 4.

ARROZ VERDE & SPANISH RICE

Green Rice & Rice with Green Chile, Olives and Tomatoes

ARROZ VERDE

This dish gets its name and color from the green of the tomatillo, jalapeño, and cilantro. ⌚⌚

3 jalapeño chiles, diced
1 (16-ounce) can tomatillos, drained
1 large garlic clove
1/4 teaspoon ground cumin
1 1/2 cups chicken broth
2 tablespoons vegetable oil
1/2 cup finely chopped onion
1 cup long-grain rice
1 tablespoon chopped fresh cilantro
Sliced jalapeño chiles

Arroz Verde (left) and Spanish Rice.

Place the chiles, tomatillos, garlic and cumin in a blender or food processor, add 1 cup of the broth, and puree the mixture until it's smooth. Add additional broth to make 2 cups of liquid.

In a heavy skillet, heat the oil over medium-high heat, add the onion, and sauté until it's soft, 2 to 3 minutes. Add the rice and sauté for a couple of minutes, or until the rice starts to turn opaque.

Bring the broth mixture to a boil in a saucepan and add the rice. Reduce the heat, cover, and simmer until all the liquid is absorbed, 20 to 30 minutes.

Remove the pan from the heat and lightly toss the rice with the chopped cilantro, garnish with the jalapeños, and serve hot. Serves 4.

SPANISH RICE ⌚

1 tablespoon vegetable oil
1 cup long-grain white rice
1 medium-size onion, chopped
1 garlic clove, minced
1 1/2 cups chicken broth
1/2 cup (about 4 to 5) roasted, peeled, seeded and chopped New Mexican green chiles
4 canned tomatoes, chopped, or 1 medium fresh tomato, peeled and chopped
1/4 cup tomato puree
1/4 cup sliced black olives
2 teaspoons dried oregano
1/4 teaspoon ground cumin
Salt
Chopped jalapeño chiles

In a heavy skillet, heat the oil over medium-high heat, add the rice, and sauté until it turns opaque and starts to brown, about 3 minutes. Stir in the onion and garlic and cook for a few more minutes.

In a saucepan over high heat, bring the broth to a boil. Add the remaining ingredients and the rice, bring back to a boil, and stir a couple of times. Reduce the heat, cover, and simmer for 20 to 30 minutes, or until the rice is tender.

Remove the rice, fluff it with a fork, and garnish with the chiles. Serve the rice hot. Makes 4 servings.

TORTILLAS & BREADS

Flour & Corn Tortillas, Flatbread, Sopaipillas, Pueblo Bread

Clockwise from top: Pueblo Oven Bread (page 109), Sopaipillas (page 108), white and blue Corn Tortillas and Flour Tortillas. These breads are served in an antique Maidu Indian winnowing tray.

FLOUR TORTILLAS ⌚⌚

2 cups all-purpose flour
½ teaspoon salt
1 teaspoon baking powder (optional)
3 to 4 tablespoons lard or vegetable shortening, or a mixture of the two
½ to ¾ cup very warm water

Sift the dry ingredients into a large bowl. Work in the shortening with your fingertips until it is evenly mixed. Pour two-thirds of the water over the mixture and mix it in with a fork. The dough will have large lumps rather than being a smooth mixture. Add the remaining water, if needed, and gather the dough into a ball.

Knead the dough well for 5 minutes. The dough should be medium stiff, not as soft as bread dough but also not firm. Divide the dough into 12 portions and roll them into balls. Cover them with a towel and let them rest for 20 minutes.

Lightly flour a board, flatten out one of the dough balls and roll it until it is thin.

Heat a dry *comal,* heavy skillet or griddle to medium hot. Lay the tortilla onto the griddle—you should hear a faint sizzle when it first hits the cooking surface. Cook until bubbles form on the top and brown spots appear underneath, 30 to 45 seconds. Turn over the tortilla and cook it for an additional 30 to 45 seconds. Be sure not to overcook it, or the tortilla will become crisp.

Remove the tortilla and cover it with a towel to keep it warm. Makes 1 dozen tortillas.

CORN TORTILLAS ⌚⌚

2 cups *masa harina*
1¼ to 1⅓ cups very warm water
½ teaspoon salt

Place the *masa harina* and the salt in a large bowl and add 1 cup of the water. Work the water in with your hands, lightly kneading the dough with the heel of your hand for 3 to 5 minutes until the mixture is smooth. Add more water if necessary. The dough should be very soft, not sticky or elastic like bread dough.

It's important that the *masa* be the right consistency. If the dough is too dry, the tortillas will be rather thick and have a grainy, crumbly edge. They also won't puff up much and will be heavy. If the dough is too wet you won't be able to form a tortilla or remove it from the plastic wrap. Both problems are easy to remedy. Just add a little more water or *masa harina,* whichever is needed.

Divide the dough into 15 portions and roll them into balls 1½ inches in diameter, cover them with plastic wrap, and let them rest for 20 to 30 minutes.

Put a sheet of plastic wrap on the bottom of a tortilla press. Place a ball of *masa* on the press, a little off-center toward the hinge. Cover the dough with another sheet of plastic wrap and press down to form the tortilla.

Heat a dry *comal,* heavy skillet, or griddle until it is medium-hot. Carefully slip the tortilla onto the *comal.* The tortilla should just sizzle as it touches the pan and shouldn't take longer than 2 minutes to cook. Turn the tortilla over and cook it slightly longer on the other side, or until it browns lightly in spots and the top begins to puff. Remove the tortilla and keep it warm in a towel for 10 to 15 minutes to let it finish cooking and become soft and pliable. Makes 15 tortillas.

ANASAZI FLATBREAD

Flynt Payne, Inn of the Anasazi

3/4 cup olive oil
8 ounces shiitake mushrooms, thinly sliced
1/4 cup finely chopped red onion
1/2 teaspoon thinly sliced fresh sage
2 1/2 cups all-purpose flour
2 tablespoons powdered dry milk
2 teaspoons baking powder
1/2 teaspoon kosher salt, plus additional salt for seasoning
3 tablespoons butter
Water

Over medium heat, sauté the mushrooms, onion and sage in 2 teaspoons of oil until they are soft. Remove them from the heat and allow them to cool.

Combine the flour, milk, baking powder and salt in the bowl of an electric mixer. Add the butter and mix it slowly with the paddle attachment until the flour mix resembles cornmeal. Slowly add water until the dough holds together and is well combined. Allow the dough to rest for 2 hours.

Roll out the dough on a lightly floured board to a thickness of 1/4 inch. Cut out 5-inch circles.

Heat the remaining oil in a skillet until it's hot, and fry the rounds until they're browned. Carefully remove them, drain them, and season them with kosher salt. Makes 12 rounds.

SOPAIPILLAS (FRIED BREAD)

Sopaipillas, or "little pillows," are squares or triangles of bread that puff up when fried. After tortillas, they are the most commonly served bread in New Mexico. They are served with traditional meals, accompanied by a dispenser of honey. The combination of the sugar in the honey and the starch of the bread cuts the heat of hot chiles. To eat the *sopaipillas,* tear or bite off a corner of the bread, pour in the honey, and enjoy.

2 cups all-purpose flour
2 teaspoons baking powder
1/2 teaspoon salt
2 tablespoons shortening
2/3 cup warm water
Vegetable oil for deep-frying

In a large bowl, combine the flour, baking powder and salt. Cut in the shortening until the flour resembles coarse meal.

Add the water, a little at a time, until the dough is moist and can be gathered into a ball. Knead it a couple of times, cover it with a towel, and let it sit for 30 minutes.

In a deep pot or fryer, heat the oil to 400°F. On a lightly floured board, roll out the dough until it forms a rectangle $\frac{1}{4}$ inch thick. Cut into rectangles about 2 by 3 inches.

Place the *sopaipillas,* 3 or 4 at a time, in the hot oil and spoon a little oil over the top of each to start them puffing. When they have browned on one side, 20 to 30 seconds, turn them over and brown the other side. Turn them only once. Remove them and drain them on paper towels.

Serve immediately. Makes 20 *sopaipillas.*

Helpful hint: For very light *sopaipillas,* do not handle the dough more than necessary.

PUEBLO OVEN BREAD

This hearty bread is baked in the adobe beehive-shaped ovens called *hornos.* Before baking, a fire is made inside the oven and is allowed to burn itself out. The ashes are swept out, the bread is placed in the oven, and the opening is sealed to allow the bread to bake. To achieve a nice crisp crust in a conventional oven, gently mist the bread with water from a spray bottle a couple of times as it bakes.

1 package active dry yeast
2 cups warm water
$\frac{1}{2}$ teaspoon sugar
2 tablespoons melted shortening, cooled
1 teaspoon salt
$4\frac{1}{2}$ cups unbleached bread flour

In a large bowl, dissolve the yeast in $\frac{1}{2}$ cup warm water (110°F) and stir in the sugar. Let it sit for 10 minutes.

Stir the shortening and the salt into the yeast mixture. Add 1 cup of the flour and beat well. Add some of the remaining $1\frac{1}{2}$ cups warm water, then some flour, beating the mixture well after each addition. Add the remaining flour and water, alternating between wet and dry.

Turn the dough onto a lightly floured board and knead it for 10 minutes, or until the dough is smooth and elastic. Gather the dough into a ball and place it in an oiled bowl. Cover the bowl with a towel and let the dough rise in a warm place until it has doubled, about 1 hour.

Punch the dough down and knead it for 5 minutes. Divide the dough in half and place in 2 smaller oiled ovenproof bowls, turning once so the tops are oiled. Cover them with a towel and let them rise for 30 minutes.

Preheat the oven to 400°F.

Bake for 45 to 50 minutes, or until the loaves are lightly browned and sound hollow when tapped. Makes 2 loaves.

CORNBREAD & CHILE-FLAVORED BUTTERS

JALAPEÑO CHEDDAR CORNBREAD

Heating the chiles in the milk takes away some of their bite, but if the bread is too spicy for you, decrease the amount of chile or substitute a milder New Mexican green chile. For mild bread, green or red bell peppers may be used.

1½ cups buttermilk
3 tablespoons (2 to 3) finely chopped jalapeño chiles
1 cup minced onion (1 large onion)
1 cup yellow cornmeal
1 cup all-purpose flour
2 teaspoons sugar
1 teaspoon baking soda
1 teaspoon baking powder
1 teaspoon salt
¼ teaspoon garlic powder
2 eggs, beaten
1 cup (4 ounces) grated cheddar cheese

Preheat the oven to 400°F and lightly oil a 9 x 9-inch pan. In a small saucepan over low heat, cook the jalapeños and onion in the buttermilk for a few minutes. Remove the pan from the heat and allow the mixture to cool.

In a large mixing bowl, combine all the dry ingredients. Mix the eggs and cheese together in another bowl. Stir in the buttermilk mixture.

Pour the liquid ingredients into the dry ones and quickly mix them. Pour the batter into the oiled pan. Bake for 40 minutes, or until it turns golden brown, and a toothpick inserted in the center comes out clean.

Cool the cornbread slightly, slice it, and serve, hot or at room temperature, accompanied by a flavored butter. Makes 9 (3-inch) pieces.

CHILE-FLAVORED BUTTERS

These compound butters can be used in a variety of ways. They keep indefinitely in the freezer, so keep several on hand.

Orange Zest Red Chile Butter

2 tablespoons grated orange zest
2 teaspoons orange juice
2 teaspoons ground red chile, such as New Mexican, *piquín* or *chile de Árbol*
1 pound (4 sticks) unsalted butter, softened

Roasted Green Chile and Spring Onion Butter

3 New Mexican green chiles, roasted, peeled, seeded and finely chopped
4 scallions, finely sliced, some of the greens included
¼ teaspoon garlic powder
1 pound (4 sticks) unsalted butter, softened

Combine all the ingredients in a bowl and mix them thoroughly. Allow the butter to sit at room temperature for 1 hour to blend the flavors.
Chill the butter before serving. Makes 1 pound.

CAJETA SUNDAE WITH TOASTED PIÑON COOKIE

Andrew MacLauchlan, Coyote Cafe

The distinctive adobe rooftops of Santa Fe as seen from the Coyote Cafe

Cajeta is a rich caramel sauce made with goat's milk; it keeps almost indefinitely if refrigerated.

Cajeta Caramel

1 quart evaporated goat's milk
$1\frac{1}{2}$ cups milk
4 teaspoons cornstarch
$\frac{1}{2}$ teaspoon baking soda
$1\frac{1}{2}$ cups sugar

Piñon Cookie

$\frac{1}{4}$ cup butter
$\frac{1}{4}$ cup brown sugar
$\frac{1}{4}$ cup sugar
$\frac{3}{4}$ cup piñon nuts, lightly roasted and ground
1 egg
$\frac{1}{2}$ teaspoon vanilla
$\frac{1}{2}$ teaspoon baking soda
6 tablespoons flour

1 quart vanilla ice cream

To make the **cajeta caramel**, combine both milks in a large saucepan and bring to a boil over medium-high heat. Reduce the heat and simmer.

In a small bowl, stir together the cornstarch and baking soda and whisk in some of the hot milk, stirring until the cornstarch mixture has dissolved. Whisk this mixture back into the milk and continue to simmer.

In another saucepan, heat the sugar over high heat, stirring continuously as it melts and turns brown (caramelizes), about 8 to 10 minutes. Reduce the heat to medium and continue to stir until the sugar is evenly melted, is a deep amber color, and is smoking lightly.

Ladle the hot milk into the caramel; be very careful because the mixture will bubble up violently. Stir the milk in until the mixture no longer bubbles up when the hot milk is added. Return this caramel-and-milk mixture to the other saucepan and simmer to reduce it by about one half, approximately 1 hour. Cool the mixture over ice.

Preheat the oven to 350°F. To make the **piñon cookie**, cream the butter and both sugars together in a mixing bowl. Add the piñon nuts, egg, vanilla, baking soda and flour and mix thoroughly.

Spread the batter into the desired shapes, about $\frac{1}{16}$ inch thick, on a nonstick baking pan with a spatula. Bake the cookies for 12 to 14 minutes, remove from the oven, and let them cool.

To serve, place a cookie on each plate and stack 2 scoops of the ice cream on top. Drizzle the plate and ice cream with the cajeta caramel. Stick another piñon cookie in the ice cream and serve. Serves 6.

ARROZ CON LECHE

Maurice Zeck, La Fonda

The banana sauce and spiced peaches that accompany this *arroz con leche* make it unique. ⌚⌚⌚

Toasted Banana Sauce

1 banana
1 pint half-and-half
2 tablespoons sugar
1 egg yolk
1 tablespoon banana liqueur

Spiced Peaches

4 fresh peaches, sliced
1 teaspoon ground cinnamon
1 tablespoon brown sugar
Pinch of ground nutmeg
2 tablespoons peach schnapps

Rice Pudding

1/4 cup raisins
2 tablespoons brandy
3/4 cup rice
2 1/2 cups milk
1 cinnamon stick, 2 to 3 inches long
Zest of 1 large lemon, peeled in wide strips
2 tablespoons vanilla
3 tablespoons brown sugar
2 egg yolks
2 tablespoons sugar

To make the **banana sauce**, preheat the oven to 400°F. Place the banana on a baking sheet and toast it in the oven until it is browned. Place it in a blender or food processor and puree until smooth.

In a saucepan over medium heat, combine the half-and-half and 1 1/2 tablespoons of the sugar. Heat until just below boiling and remove from the heat.

In a small bowl, whisk the egg yolk with the remaining sugar. Add 2 tablespoons of the hot half-and-half to temper the yolks. Stir the yolk mixture into the rest of the half-and-half. Return the saucepan to the heat and cook until the mixture coats the back of a spoon. Stir in the liqueur. Remove the mixture from the heat, add the banana puree, and mix well. Refrigerate the sauce for 1 hour, or until it is well chilled.

To prepare the **peaches**, combine all the ingredients, toss well, and set aside.

To make the pudding, put the raisins in a bowl and cover them with the brandy to plump them. Combine the rice, milk, cinnamon, lemon zest, vanilla and brown sugar in a medium saucepan. Simmer over low heat, covered, until the rice is cooked, 12 to 15 minutes. When the rice is done, remove the cinnamon stick and lemon zest. Add the brandy and raisins to the mixture.

Whisk together the egg yolks and the rest of the sugar and stir the mixture into the rice. Continue to cook the rice, stirring often for 5 to 10 minutes, until thickened. Be careful not to overcook.

Place the pudding in a glass serving bowl, drizzle banana sauce over the top, and garnish with the peaches. Serves 4.

Capriotada (left, recipe on page 136) and Arroz con Leche

TACO-NOLIS

Katharine Kagel, Cafe Pasqual's

These are a Santa Fe takeoff on cannoli, the renowned Italian dessert. This dessert is shaped like a taco. The tequila-flavored ricotta is topped with pistachio nuts to imitate the avocado, dried cherries for tomatoes, chocolate chips for the ground beef, and colored coconut to represent lettuce and cheese. Delicious and hilarious! ⌚⌚⌚

Shells

1 tablespoon sugar
1½ tablespoons butter
2 cups all-purpose flour
1 egg yolk
¼ cup white wine
3 cups canola oil

Filling

2 cups ricotta cheese, drained
¾ cup powdered sugar
1½ cups heavy whipping cream
½ teaspoon vanilla
1½ tablespoons tequila

Topping

10 to 12 fresh cherries, or 2 tablespoons dried cherries
1 package shredded coconut
Orange and green food coloring
⅓ cup pistachios
1 package tiny chocolate chips

For the **shells**, blend the sugar and butter with the flour and add the egg yolk and white wine. Divide the dough into 10 pieces and roll each into a ball. Using a pasta machine, roll out the dough into thin rounds about 5 to 6 inches in diameter.

In a stockpot or fryer, heat the oil to 370°F, or until a pinch of dough dropped into the oil bobs to the surface immediately. Drape the dough over a taco, or use tongs to fold the dough in half, keeping it open enough for the filling, and fry the shell until it's golden brown. Drain the taco-noli and set it aside on paper towels to absorb any oil.

For the **filling**, whisk together the ricotta and sugar. Using an electric mixer, whip the cream until it's stiff. Fold the vanilla and tequila carefully into the whipped cream. Fold in the ricotta. Refrigerate the mixture until you're ready to fill the taco-nolis.

To make the **toppings**, pit and destem the cherries and cut them into quarters. Mix ½ cup of the coconut with 2 or 3 drops of orange food coloring to make the "cheese," and mix another ½ cup of coconut with 2 or 3 drops of green food coloring for the "lettuce"; toss to color the coconut. Rub the skin off the pistachios to make the "avocado."

Spoon the filling into the tacos and sprinkle on the toppings. Serve immediately. Makes 10 "tacos."

NATILLAS

Santa Fe School of Cooking

This dish is similar to the classic French dessert "floating islands"—a rich custard with spoonfuls of meringue on top—though with some differences. In Santa Fe, the meringue is folded into the custard, which is then stabilized with flour. This technique was originally used to extend eggs, an item that was in short supply for the early Santa Fe settlers. ⌚⌚

Natillas (left) and Vanilla Flan (page 135).

2 eggs, separated
2 tablespoons flour
2 cups heavy cream, divided
¼ cup plus 2 tablespoons sugar, divided
Pinch of salt
¾ teaspoon vanilla, preferably Mexican
Freshly grated nutmeg or cinnamon

In a bowl, make a paste of the egg yolks, flour and ½ cup of the cream.

In a saucepan, combine ¼ cup of the sugar and the salt with the remaining cream and bring the mixture to just below boiling.

Whisk the scalded cream gradually into the egg mixture then place it in a double boiler over simmering water. Cook the mixture slowly, stirring constantly, until it thickens, about 20 minutes.

Mix in the vanilla and let the mixture cool. The recipe may be made ahead of time to this point.

Beat the egg whites with the remaining 2 tablespoons of sugar until they're stiff and shiny but not dry. Fold the egg whites into the cooled custard.

Sprinkle with freshly grated nutmeg or cinnamon and serve immediately. Serves 4 to 6.

EMPANADITAS WITH APRICOT PECAN FILLING

Dessert Turnovers

Empanaditas are little filled pies, or turnovers, that are found in one form or another all around the world. These may be baked with or without a sugar topping, or deep-fried and dusted with powdered sugar before serving. The filling may be pureed or left with some texture. If you do puree it, do so before adding nuts and eliminate the raisins. ⌚⌚

Filling

1 pound dried apricots, cut into quarters
1 cup sugar, or more to taste
½ teaspoon salt
¼ teaspoon ground nutmeg
¼ cup raisins
¼ cup chopped pecans

Dough

2 cups all-purpose flour
1 teaspoon salt
⅔ cup vegetable shortening
4 to 5 tablespoons cold water
1 egg, separated

To make the **filling**, place the apricots in a saucepan over medium heat and cover them with water. Add the sugar and simmer until the apricots are very soft and start to break down, 20 to 25 minutes. Add more water if necessary. Stir in the remaining ingredients, remove the pan from the heat, and allow the filling to cool.

Preheat the oven to 400°F.

To make the **dough**, combine the flour and salt in a large mixing bowl. Cut the shortening into the dry ingredients using a pastry cutter or two forks. The mixture should resemble coarse cornmeal.

Add 4 to 5 tablespoons of cold water, one tablespoon at a time, and lightly toss with a fork to incorporate it. Add only enough water for the dough to hold together and be gathered into a ball.

Lightly beat the white. Beat the yolk separately with 1 tablespoon of water.

To make the crust, gently roll out the dough on a lightly floured surface to a thickness of ¼ inch and use a round cookie cutter or juice glass to cut circles 2 to 2½ inches in diameter. Place a spoonful of the filling off-center on each circle. Brush the edges with the egg white, fold in half, and crimp the edges to seal it.

Brush the *empanaditas* with the egg yolk, place them on a lightly oiled baking pan, and bake them for 10 to 12 minutes, or until golden.

Remove them and cool them on a rack before serving. Makes 2 dozen.

Helpful hint: If you're short on time, ready-made pie crusts may be used for the pastry, but don't roll out the pastry before cutting it.

GRANITA

Kelly Rogers, La Casa Sena

Granitas are intentionally made to have a grainy texture similar to shaved ice. This frozen fruit ice is a popular choice at La Casa Sena and may be served as an intermezzo (something eaten between courses to cleanse the palate), a dessert or even a cocktail! It's so easy to make, you'll be laughing as your guests are praising you. This recipe is for three different *granitas;* use a different juice for each one. ⌚

Beat the desert heat with granita served in whimsical cactus glasses.

Simple Syrup

1/3 cup sugar
2/3 cup water

2 cups fresh watermelon juice, grapefruit juice or prickly pear cactus juice
1 jalapeño chile, seeded and finely chopped
Juice of half a lime
4 sprigs of mint

To make the **simple syrup**, combine the sugar and the water in a small saucepan. Simmer over low heat until the sugar has dissolved and the mixture is clear. Raise the heat and boil for 1 minute.

Combine the fruit juice, jalapeño, simple syrup and lime juice in a saucepan and simmer for 5 minutes over medium heat to incorporate the simple syrup. Do not boil or reduce the sauce.

Pour the mixture into a shallow metal dish and place it in the freezer. Every hour, stir the mixture to cause ice crystals to form. After a few hours, the granita will form into a granular substance similar to shaved ice.

Serve the *granita* in chilled martini glasses with a sprig of mint. If you feel daring, splash a little tequila, vodka or champagne over it and serve it as a cocktail. Serves 4.

Helpful hint: To juice a watermelon, place the "meat" of the melon in a medium-mesh strainer and force it through with a ladle or wooden spoon into a bowl.

MARIA'S MARGARITAS

Al Lucero, Maria's New Mexican Kitchen

The origin of the margarita is uncertain, but many stories are told. One is that a bartender in Palm Springs invented it just after World War II and named it after his girlfriend. Another is that in the late forties a woman named Margarita Sames concocted it while throwing a party for friends at her hacienda in Acapulco. Yet another claims that the owner of a Los Angeles bar and restaurant called the Tail o'the Cock was the originator. He was, by coincidence, a guest at Margarita's bash in Mexico. No matter who created the drink, it is responsible for the United States becoming the largest consumer of tequila. We import more than double what is drunk in Mexico! Maria's New Mexican Kitchen is well known for serving the most authentic and best margaritas—at least according to Robert Redford.

A sampling of margaritas—both elegant and bold—at Maria's New Mexican Kitchen.

MARIA'S SPECIAL MARGARITA

Maria's Special Margarita is touted as the best-selling hand-shaken margarita in Santa Fe.

1 lemon or lime wedge
Saucer of kosher salt, about 1/4 inch deep
1 1/4 ounces Jose Cuervo Silver tequila
3/4 ounce Bols triple sec
1 1/2 ounces freshly squeezed lemon juice or lime juice

Rub the lemon or lime wedge around the rim of a margarita glass. Dip the rim of the glass into the saucer of salt and rotate it until the salt has collected on the glass.

Pour the tequila, triple sec and juice into a 16-ounce cocktail shaker glass full of ice. Place the shaker over the glass and shake it for about 5 seconds. Pour the drink into the salted glass and serve immediately. Makes 1 margarita.

THE ELIZABETH II

This drink was created one night after a waitress described the ingredients of a margarita to a customer. He was a fan of orange liqueurs and asked if they could be substituted or included. They were, and a new margarita was born. The name Elizabeth II refers to the waitress and the two orange liqueurs.

1 lemon or lime wedge
Saucer of kosher salt, about 1/4 inch deep
1 1/4 ounces El Tesoro Plata tequila
1/2 ounce Grand Marnier
1/2 ounce Cointreau
1 1/2 ounces freshly squeezed lemon juice or lime juice

Rub the lemon or lime wedge around the rim of a margarita glass. Dip the rim of the glass into the

TRIPLE
RESERVA

saucer of salt and rotate it until the salt has collected on the glass.

Pour the tequila, Grand Marnier, Cointreau and juice into a 16-ounce cocktail shaker glass full of ice. Place a stainless-steel cocktail shaker over the glass and shake it vigorously for about 5 seconds. Pour the drink into the salted glass and serve immediately. Makes 1 margarita.

EL AMOR DE ORO MARGARITA

This drink, named "The Golden Love," is one of the most elegant margaritas served at Maria's.

1 lemon or lime wedge
Saucer of kosher salt, about 1/4 inch deep
1 1/4 ounces Centinela 100 Percent Blue Agave Tres Años tequila
3/4 ounce Cointreau
1 1/2 ounces freshly squeezed lemon juice or lime juice

Rub the lemon or lime wedge around the rim of a margarita glass. Dip the rim of the glass into the saucer of salt and rotate it until the salt has collected on the glass.

Pour the tequila, Cointreau and juice into a 16-ounce cocktail shaker glass full of ice. Place a stainless-steel cocktail shaker over the glass and shake it vigorously for about 5 seconds. Pour the drink into the salted glass and serve immediately. Makes 1 margarita.

MARIA'S FAMOUS LA ULTIMA MARGARITA

Up until the time this margarita was created, most tequila connoisseurs would only drink super-premium tequila straight. To get the full flavor of this drink, there should be no substitutions.

1 lemon or lime wedge
Saucer of kosher salt, about 1/4 inch deep
1 1/4 ounces El Tesoro 100 Percent Blue Agave Plata tequila
3/4 ounce Cointreau
1 1/2 ounces freshly squeezed lemon or lime juice

Rub the lemon or lime wedge around the rim of a margarita glass. Dip the rim of the glass into the saucer of salt and rotate it until the salt has collected on the glass.

Pour the tequila, Cointreau and juice into a 16-ounce cocktail shaker glass full of ice. Place a stainless-steel cocktail shaker over the glass and shake it vigorously for about 5 seconds. Pour the drink into the salted glass and serve immediately. Makes 1 margarita.

24-KARAT GOLD RESERVE

Three hundred and fifty years in the making! This combination of 200th Anniversary Hand Crafted Jose Cuervo Añejo 100% Agave Barrel Select tequila and 150th Anniversary Cuveé Speciale Grand Marnier are the basis of the "most elegant Margarita in the world."

1 lemon or lime wedge
$1\frac{1}{4}$ ounces 200th Anniversary Hand Crafted Jose Cuervo Añejo 100% Agave Barrel Select tequila
$\frac{3}{4}$ ounce 150th Anniversary Cuveé Speciale Grand Marnier
$1\frac{1}{2}$ ounce lemon or lime juice

Rub the lemon or lime wedge around the rim of a margarita glass. Dip the rim of the glass into the saucer of salt and rotate it until the salt has collected on the glass.

Pour the tequila, Grand Marnier and juice into a 16-ounce cocktail shaker glass full of ice. Place a stainless-steel cocktail shaker over the glass and shake it vigorously for about 5 seconds. Pour the drink into the salted glass and serve immediately. Makes 1 margarita.

CHIMAYÓ COCKTAIL

Chimayó is a small village just north of Santa Fe that was settled by the Spanish in the seventeenth century. It's famous for its chile, apples and the healing properties of the holy dirt that is found in the *santuario* (church) in the village. Every Easter, thousands of people from all over the state make a pilgrimage and walk to the shrine in Chimayó. The Jaramillo family, which owns the picturesque Rancho de Chimayó restaurant, invented this cocktail to promote both the village and its apples.

$1\frac{1}{4}$ ounces tequila
$\frac{1}{4}$ ounce crème de cassis
1 ounce fresh apple cider or apple juice
$\frac{1}{4}$ ounce freshly squeezed lemon juice
1 red apple wedge

Fill a double old-fashioned glass with ice. Pour the tequila, crème de cassis, apple cider and lemon juice over the ice and stir. Garnish the glass with an apple wedge and serve. Makes 1 cocktail.

Appendix

PREPARING CHILE RELLENOS

***Step 1**: Peel a roasted chile, then make a slit near the top and remove the seeds through it. Stuff it with the filling.*

***Step 2:** Roll the chile in flour then shake off the excess flour.*

***Step 3:** Dip the chile in the batter. Fry it in oil, turning it once so it browns on both sides. Drain on paper towels.*

Chiles rellenos literally means "stuffed chiles," and any chile that is large enough to stuff can be used. In Mexico the most common chile used is the poblano, but many others—jalapeños, dried anchos and chipotles—are also popular. In the Southwest, the green New Mexican is the chile of choice.

If you use fresh chiles, they need to be roasted then peeled and seeded (see pages 30–31), leaving the stem and the flesh of the chile intact. Dried chiles must be soaked and drained before stuffing.

Just as you can use any chile that can be stuffed, any filling that you can get into that chile will work. The simplest and most popular one is cheese, most commonly cheddar, but any type of soft cheese is fine. Keep in mind that whatever filling you use needs to be firm enough to not leak out during cooking. Meat or fish must be precooked because the frying time is not long enough to cook the filling.

To fill the chile (see recipes on pages 68 and 72), make a slit near the top large enough for you to remove the seeds and put in the stuffing. Fill the chile but don't pack it too full; you want be able to close the chile before dipping it in the flour and batter. If you need to, overlap the sides along the slit, holding them together with a toothpick. Just remember to remove them before serving.

Coat the chiles well with batter, as the coating prevents the chile from absorbing oil. For frying, the oil must be hot enough so the coating will cook and brown quickly. If the chiles sit too long, they absorb too much oil and become soggy and greasy.

Slide the chiles, a couple at a time, into the hot oil. As they are browning, carefully spoon some of the hot oil on top to set the batter. Brown both sides, turning only once. Remove and drain the chiles. Serve hot with or without a sauce or salsa on top.

MAKING A TAMALE: METHOD 1

Step 1: *Soak the corn husks in water to soften them. Spread the masa on the husk and place the filling on the masa.*

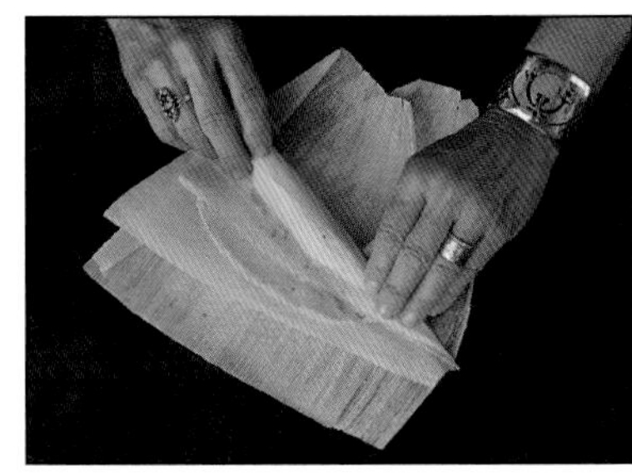

Step 2: *Fold the husk around the masa and the filling.*

Step 3: *Use two strips of leftover corn husks to tie the tamale at both ends.*

MAKING A TAMALE: METHOD 2

Step 1: *To make a squarer tamale, soak the corn husks, then spread on the masa and the filling.*

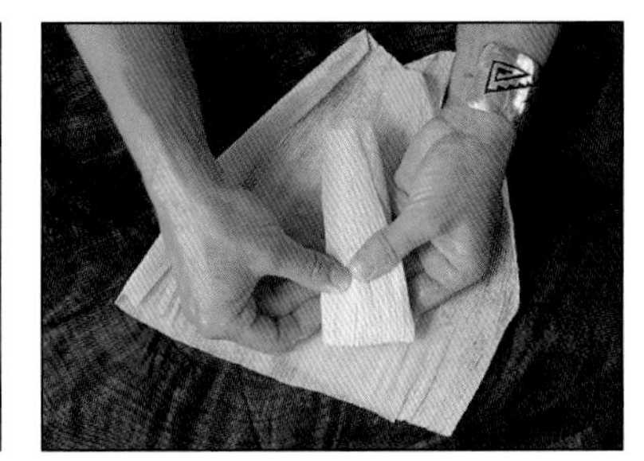

Step 2: *Fold up the husk and fold the tapered end over the filled husk.*

Step 3: *Fold the other end over the filled husk and tie it around the middle with a strip of corn husk.*

Tamales are small corn husk packages that are filled with corn masa and lard or shortening. They are flavored with a wide variety of ingredients, including cheese, beans, chiles, beef, chicken and fish. They are typically steamed. Tamales freeze well and can be steamed to reheat them, so you may want to make them in large quantities.

Tamales can be tied two ways, both illustrated above. For these tamales dried corn husks that have been soaked are used. In some Mexican versions, tender fresh corn husks are used.

Once they are folded, steam the tamales. They are ready when the filling is firm and comes away from the corn husk easily.

Additional Recipes

POSOLE
(Pork and Posole Corn)

See the photograph on page 4. Treating corn with lime to remove the tough skins was probably a technique the early Meso-American cultures passed on to the Pueblo Indians in New Mexico. The corn that is used is the same kind used to make hominy, but the processing imparts a different taste. This corn, called *posole,* is the main ingredient of this dish of the same name. It is traditionally served during the Christmas season, when a pot simmering on the stove provides welcoming fare for holiday well-wishers. Hominy corn can be substituted for the posole corn, although the taste will be different. 🕒🕒🕒

3/4 cup dried posole
1 pound lean pork, cut into 1½-inch cubes
1 to 2 tablespoons vegetable oil
1 large onion, diced
2 garlic cloves, minced
2 cups pork or chicken broth
2 to 3 tablespoons ground New Mexican red chile
1 teaspoon dried oregano
Salt

Garnish

Chopped fresh cilantro
Diced onions
Basic Red Chile Sauce (page 39)
4–6 flour tortillas

In a large saucepan or stockpot, cover the posole with water and soak it overnight.

The next day, bring the water and posole to a boil, reduce the heat, and simmer until the kernels start to become tender, 1 to 1½ hours. Add more water if necessary.

In a heavy skillet, brown the pork over medium-high heat, adding a little oil if needed. When the pork is browned, add it to the posole. Add the onions to the skillet and, if needed, additional oil. Sauté the onions until they turn a golden brown, 5 to 10 minutes. Add the garlic and cook for an additional minute. Transfer the mixture to the stockpot with the posole.

Add the pork broth to the skillet, raise the heat, and deglaze, being sure to scrape all the bits and pieces from the sides and bottom. Pour the broth into the posole.

Add the chile and oregano to the stockpot and salt to taste. Bring it to just below boiling, reduce the heat and simmer for 1 to 1½ hours, or until the meat is very tender and starts to fall apart. Add more broth or water if necessary.

Place the garnishes in small serving bowls, ladle the stew into large soup bowls, and serve immediately with warm flour tortillas. Serves 4 to 6.

CHICOS
(Dried Corn Stew)

See the photograph on page 4. *Chicos* are corn that has been steamed before drying. You will need to soak the chicos overnight for this recipe. ⌚⌚⌚

1 cup dried chicos
2 teaspoons vegetable oil
1 large onion, diced
1 garlic clove, minced
$1\frac{1}{2}$ teaspoons dried oregano, preferably Mexican
2 dried New Mexican red chile pods, crushed
Salt
Basic Red Chile Sauce (page 39)
4–6 flour tortillas

In a large saucepan or stockpot, cover the chicos with water and soak them overnight. Bring the water and chicos to a boil, reduce the heat, and cook until the kernels start to become tender, 1 to 2 hours. Add more water if necessary.

In a heavy skillet over medium heat, add the oil and onion and sauté until golden brown, 5 to 10 minutes. Add the garlic and cook for another minute. Transfer the mixture to the pot with the chicos.

Add a cup of water to the skillet, raise the heat, and deglaze, scraping all the bits and pieces from the sides and bottom. Pour the water into the chicos. Add the oregano to the stockpot and continue to cook for another hour, or until the chicos are tender. Add the crushed chile, add salt to taste, and simmer for 5 minutes. To serve, ladle the chicos into bowls and accompany them with warm flour tortillas. Serves 4 to 6.

CHIPOTLE BEEF AND BEAN BURRITOS

See the photograph on page 91. Burritos, or "little burros," are flour tortillas that are wrapped or folded around a filling. This is one of the most common uses of flour tortillas. Any of the fillings for tacos can be used, and burritos may be smothered in a chile sauce or folded up and eaten as a sandwich. Breakfast burritos filled with scrambled eggs, potatoes, bacon, sausage (or chorizo) and served with a chile sauce are one of our most popular "fast foods." ⌚⌚⌚

4 flour tortillas
2 cups Chipotle Sauce (page 40)
2 cups Refried Beans (page 86)
1 cup Beef Filling (page 86)
1 cup (4 ounces) grated cheddar cheese

Soften the tortillas by wrapping them in a cloth towel and heating them in the microwave for 20 seconds on high or by placing them on a hot comal for a minute or two.

To assemble, lay the tortilla on a flat surface and ladle on some of the sauce, spread a layer of beans over the sauce, and top with some beef and cheese.

Fold up one end of the tortilla about 1 inch over the filling. Next, fold the right and left sides over the folded end, overlapping one of the sides, and finally fold down the remaining end.

Serve with or without additional sauce over the top. Serves 4.

MEXICAN CORN CHOWDER

Rosalea Murphy, Pink Adobe Restaurant

See the photograph on page 63.

1/4 pound butter (1 stick)
1/2 cup (about 5 ounces) sliced mushrooms
1 green bell pepper, diced
1 large onion, diced
1 jalapeño chile, diced
1 teaspoon cumin seed
3/4 cup all-purpose flour
1 teaspoon ground paprika
1 teaspoon ground red pepper
1 quart chicken broth
2 cups half-and-half
1/2 cup (2 ounces) grated cheddar cheese
1 (17-ounce) can whole-kernel corn
1 tablespoon chopped fresh parsley
1 tablespoon diced pimiento
Salt

Heat a large saucepan over medium heat, add 2 tablespoons of the butter, sauté the mushrooms until they're browned, 3 to 4 minutes, remove, and reserve them.

Add the remaining butter to the saucepan, add the bell pepper, onion, jalapeño and cumin seed and sauté until they're soft, about 3 to 5 minutes. Whisk in the flour, paprika and red pepper and mix well to eliminate any lumps that may form.

Reduce the heat to low, stir in the chicken broth, and mix well. Add the half-and-half and the cheese and stir continuously until the cheese has melted and the soup has thickened.

Add the corn, parsley, pimiento and the reserved mushrooms; mix well; and heat thoroughly. Salt to taste and serve immediately. Serves 4 to 6.

BLUE CORN CHIMAYÓ CHILE BACON MUFFINS

See the photograph on page 67. Three distinctive flavors combine and complement one another in these muffins—the saltiness of the bacon, the nutty flavor of the blue corn and a subtle chile heat that is not immediately discernable.

4 to 5 strips bacon
1/4 cup blue cornmeal
1 cup all-purpose flour
1/3 cup sugar
3 teaspoons baking powder
1 teaspoon ground red Chimayó chile
3/4 teaspoon salt
1 cup milk
1 egg, beaten
2 tablespoons butter, melted, or bacon drippings

Preheat the oven to 425°F.

Fry the bacon in a skillet until it's crisp. Remove the bacon, drain it on a paper towel, and crumble it. Reserve the drippings for the muffins.

In a large mixing bowl, sift together the cornmeal, flour, sugar, baking powder, chile and salt. Set the mixture aside.

In another bowl, combine the milk, egg, butter or drippings and bacon. Add the liquid to the dry ingredients and stir to just mix them.

Lightly oil a muffin pan and divide the batter evenly among 12 to 15 muffin cups, filling up each one about halfway. Bake for 15 to 20 minutes.

Cool the muffins on a rack and serve them warm or at room temperature. Makes 12 to 15 muffins.

VENISON RED CHILE STEW

See the photograph on page 71. When you order "chili" in Santa Fe, you will be served a variation of this recipe, not a soupy bean dish. It is a recipe that has its roots in old Pueblo Indian cooking and is basically meat in a seasoned chile sauce. Pork and beef are more commonly used, but venison is a tasty variation. ⌚⌚⌚

6 to 8 dried New Mexican red chiles
1 ancho chile
1 pasilla chile (optional)
2 tablespoons vegetable oil
2 pounds venison, cut into 1½-inch cubes
1 large onion, chopped
3 garlic cloves, minced
3 cups beef broth
Salt

Preheat the oven to 250°F.

Place the chiles on a baking pan and toast for 15 minutes, or until fragrant, being careful not to let them burn. Remove the stems and seeds from the chiles and crumble them into a bowl. Cover them with hot water and let them steep 15 minutes, until soft (see page 31). Drain them and discard the water.

In a heavy skillet, heat the oil over medium heat, add the venison, and brown. Remove the meat and add the onion to the pan. Add more oil if necessary and sauté until the onion begins to brown, 5 to 10 minutes. Add the garlic and cook for 1 to 2 minutes.

Place the chiles and onion mixture in a blender or food processor. Add 1 cup of the broth and puree until smooth, adding more broth if necessary. Strain the mixture through a sieve.

In a large saucepan, combine the chile mixture, venison, and remaining broth. Bring it to just below boiling, reduce the heat, and simmer until the meat is very tender and the sauce has thickened, 1 to 1½ hours. Serves 4 to 6.

SANTA FE COLESLAW
Santa Fe School of Cooking

See the photograph on page 83. ⌚⌚

1 pound green cabbage, shredded
1 medium-size cucumber, peeled, seeded and cut in thin diagonal slices
5 scallions, thinly sliced on the diagonal
1 medium-size red bell pepper, julienned
1 medium-size yellow bell pepper, julienned
2 celery ribs, thinly sliced on the diagonal
1 large carrot, shredded
1 small white onion, cut into thin slivers (optional)

Dressing
¼ cup lime juice, preferably fresh
2 tablespoons cider vinegar
1 teaspoon to 1 tablespoon hot pepper sauce
¼ cup sugar
1 teaspoon salt

In a large mixing bowl, combine the cabbage, cucumber, scallions, bell peppers, celery, carrot and onion.

In a small bowl, combine the dressing ingredients and stir them until the sugar has dissolved.

Pour the dressing over the vegetables and toss well. Let the mixture stand at room temperature for at least 30 minutes, tossing often, before serving.

For maximum color and flavor, serve within 3 to 4 hours. Serves 6.

PICKLED RED ONIONS
Santa Fe School of Cooking

See the photograph on page 83. ***Note:*** This recipe requires advance preparation.

2 cups red wine vinegar
1 (6-ounce) can frozen orange juice concentrate, thawed
$^3/_4$ cup sugar
1 tablespoon dried oregano, preferably Mexican
4 bay leaves, broken in half
Salt
$1^1/_4$ pounds medium-size red onions (about 6), cut into slivers

Combine all the ingredients, except the onions, in a large nonreactive bowl and stir them until the sugar has dissolved. Add the onions and combine them well. Cover the bowl and let the mixture stand at room temperature, stirring occasionally, for 12 to 24 hours. Stir the mixture once again, cover the bowl, and refrigerate.

These onions keep for up to two weeks. After that, they retain their flavor but lose some of the vibrant color. Makes 4 cups.

FIRE-ROASTED VEGETABLES
Katharine Kagel, Cafe Pasqual's

See the photograph on page 89.

Marinade

1 cup olive oil
$^1/_3$ cup balsamic vinegar
1 tablespoon minced garlic
Kosher salt
2 teaspoons freshly ground black pepper

1 large red onion, sliced into thick rounds
2 red bell peppers, seeded and cut into long strips $^1/_2$ inch wide
2 yellow squash, sliced lengthwise into $^1/_4$-inch-wide slabs
2 zucchini, sliced lengthwise into $^1/_4$-inch-wide slabs
2 Japanese eggplants, sliced lengthwise into $^1/_4$-inch-wide slabs

To prepare the marinade for the vegetables, combine the olive oil, vinegar, garlic, salt and pepper in a bowl. Place all the vegetables in a shallow nonreactive bowl and pour the marinade over the top, coating each piece well. Marinate at room temperature for 4 to 6 hours.

Prepare a fire in a charcoal grill. When the coals are medium-hot, add the marinated vegetables to the grill rack. Grill them, turning frequently, until they're charred, 7 to 12 minutes.

VANILLA FLAN
Santa Fe School of Cooking

See the photograph on page 119.

$1\frac{1}{4}$ cups sugar
1 cup milk
2 cups heavy cream
2 large eggs
3 large egg yolks
2 teaspoons pure vanilla extract

Preheat the oven to 325°F.

Add 1 cup of sugar to a small, dry skillet. Place the skillet over medium-high heat and melt the sugar. As the sugar caramelizes, press the unmelted sugar into the liquefied part with the bottom of a heavy spoon.

Reduce the heat to medium and continue cooking until you have a clear, deep amber liquid, 8 to 10 minutes. Remove the syrup from the heat and immediately pour equal amounts into six $\frac{1}{2}$-cup ramekins, tilting the cups to distribute the syrup evenly on the bottoms and sides.

In a saucepan over medium heat, combine the milk, cream and the remaining $\frac{1}{4}$ cup of sugar. Heat the mixture over medium-high heat until it's hot but not boiling, stirring to dissolve the sugar. Remove the pan from the heat and let the mixture cool slightly.

In a small bowl, whisk together the eggs and yolks until they're well blended. Slowly pour the eggs into the heated milk mixture, whisking constantly. Stir in the vanilla. Place the ramekins in a baking pan and divide the milk mixture among the prepared ramekins. Add boiling water to the pan to come about three-quarters of the way up the sides of the ramekins. Bake the custard in the water bath for 35 to 45 minutes, or until it no longer trembles when moved.

Remove the ramekins from the pan, cool them, and refrigerate them, covered, for 3 to 4 hours.

To serve, unmold the custard by running a knife around the edge of the ramekins and transfer the custard onto dessert plates. Serves 6.

SAFFRON RICE
Katharine Kagel, Cafe Pasqual's

See the photograph on page 89.

1 teaspoon saffron threads
$\frac{1}{4}$ cup olive oil
$\frac{1}{2}$ white onion, finely minced
2 teaspoons finely minced garlic
$1\frac{1}{2}$ teaspoons kosher salt
$\frac{1}{2}$ teaspoon white pepper
2 cups long-grain white rice

To make the rice, toast the saffron in a small, dry sauté pan over medium heat, shaking the pan continuously to prevent burning. Toast for 2 minutes, or until fragrant. Remove the saffron from the heat and reserve it.

In a large saucepan over medium heat, combine the oil, onion, garlic, salt and pepper. Stir for 1 to 2 minutes and add the rice. Stir constantly until the oil is absorbed and the rice begins to smell nutty, about 2 minutes.

Add 3 cups water to the rice, stir in the saffron, and bring to a boil over medium-high heat. Reduce the heat to low, cover the saucepan, and simmer until all the water is absorbed, 20 to 30 minutes.

CAPRIOTADA WITH RASPBERRY SAUCE AND WHIPPED CREAM
Maurice Zeck, La Fonda

See the photograph on page 115. This dessert is called by two different names—*capriotada* and *sopa.* Now made throughout the year, historically it was served only on special occasions. Traditionally it has been made with lard, but you may substitute butter.

Pudding

2 tablespoons butter or lard
3 to 4 slices stale white bread
3 ounces semisweet chocolate, melted
1/4 cup sugar
1 teaspoon ground cinnamon
2 ounces asadero cheese, finely grated
1 tablespoon chopped walnuts
1 tablespoon chopped peanuts
2 teaspoons pine nuts
1 tablespoon raisins

Raspberry sauce

2 pints fresh raspberries
1/4 cup orange juice, preferably fresh
2 tablespoons butter
2 tablespoons sugar
1 tablespoon orange liqueur (such as Cointreau)
1 tablespoon raspberry liqueur
2 tablespoons cornstarch mixed with 3 tablespoons water (optional)

Nutmeg cream

1 cup heavy cream
2 to 3 tablespoons sugar
1/2 teaspoon grated nutmeg

Preheat the oven to 250°F.

In a heavy skillet, heat the butter until it's hot, add the bread, and fry until it's golden. Remove the bread and drain it on paper towels.

In a heavy saucepan over medium-high heat, add the chocolate, sugar, cinnamon and 1 cup water. Bring it to a boil, reduce the heat, and simmer while stirring to form a syrup, about 5 minutes.

Lightly oil a 9 x 12-inch baking dish or pan. Layer the bread, cheese, syrup, nuts and raisins in the pan; cover the pan; and bake for 30 to 45 minutes, or until golden. Remove the pan and let it cool.

To make the sauce, combine all the ingredients except the cornstarch and water in a saucepan and bring it to a boil. Reduce the heat and simmer for 15 minutes. Remove and strain the sauce. If the sauce is too thin, return it to the pan, heat it, and stir in the cornstarch mixture and thicken it to the desired consistency.

Whip the cream with the sugar and nutmeg until it's thick. To assemble, place the pudding on a plate or in a bowl. Drizzle the sauce over the pudding, top with the cream, and serve at room temperature. Serves 4.

Sources

Shopping Guide

Page 4: *santo (San Rafael)* by Marie Romero Cash, spoon painted by Paula Summers.

Page 27: dippers from Griffith Ranch Trading Company.

Page 40: Kachina-inspired figurine from La Mesa of Santa Fe by Gregory Lomayesva; bowls from Gift n Gourmet; woven basket from Glen Green Galleries.

Page 41: metal sauce bowl from Nambé.

Page 42: salt and pepper shakers from Merry Elizabeth Foss.

Page 43: woven cloth from Merry Elizabeth Foss.

Page 45: platter and cup from Merry Elizabeth Foss; wood bowl and spatula from the Santa Fe School of Cooking and Market.

Page 47: steel cowboy hat by Emilio Romero, Jr.; pewter platter from Gift n Gourmet; place mat from Cookworks.

Page 48: handmade plate from Kelly Jo Designs by Kelly Jo Kuchar; glasses from Cookworks; napkin ring from Nambé.

Page 51: plate and metal charger from Nambé; fork from Casa Ana by Megin Diamond.

Page 53: plate from La Mesa of Santa Fe; napkin from The Chile Shop; stool by Daryl Griffith from Griffith Ranch Trading Company; tiger head from Davis and Christine Mather.

Page 55: handmade serving bowls in traditional floral designs from Galería Hispánica; lamp and recycled wood and iron feathered table from Griffith Ranch Trading Company.

Page 59: kinetic steel sculpture in the Coyote Cafe's rooftop cantina by Fredrick Prescot.

Page 61: soup bowl and plate from La Mesa of Santa Fe; wood inlay spoon from Cutlery of Santa Fe.

Page 63: bowls from Santa Fe Pottery; treble clef spoon from Cookworks.

Page 65: glasses from Cookworks; spoon from Gift n Gourmet.

Page 67: plate from La Mesa of Santa Fe; Bolivian *manta,* or shawl, from Merry Elizabeth Foss; handcrafted belt by Eduardo Fuss; radio set and table made of recycled wood, vinyl and linoleum by James Holmes.

Page 69: plate, horn knife and fork from Cookworks; antique Mexican cloth from Nathalie.

Page 71: wooden plate from Santa Fe Pottery.

Page 73: plate from In Home Furnishings; silver fork and napkins from Cookworks; painted canvas from Trompe Deluxe by Elaine Roy and Karen Browne.

Page 75: utensils and glass from Cookworks; table painted by Rosalea Murphy.

Page 77: wooden platter and basket from Santa Fe School of Cooking and Market; wood inlay fork and spoon from Cutlery of Santa Fe.

Page 79: platter from La Mesa of Santa Fe by Rob Sanders; canvas from Trompe Deluxe by Elaine Roy and Karen Browne.

Page 81: plate by Heidi Loewen; table linens from Cookworks.

Page 83: ceramic plate from Rainbow Gate; bowls, plates and servers from Santa Fe School of Cooking and Market.

Page 85: plate, charger, knife and fork from Cookworks; stool made of recycled linoleum, wood, lead and buffalo horns by James Holmes.

Page 87: platters from Santa Fe Pottery.

Page 89: traditional folk ranch dinner plate from Merry Elizabeth Foss.

Page 91: servers from James Reid, Ltd.; table and stool boxes from African Odyssey; serving platter from La Mesa of Santa Fe.

Page 93: plate from Rainbow Gate; cutlery and glass from Cookworks; salt and pepper shaker from Nambé; bolo napkin tie from James Reid Ltd.

Page 95: plates from The Chile Shop; Native American basket from Glen Green Galleries; napkins, napkin rings and table from African Odyssey.

Page 97: Kokopelli table from Seckler Studio; plate from La Mesa of Santa Fe; twig cutlery from Cookworks.

Page 99: Peruvian silver utensils from Casa Ana; table from Tinwork Studio and Gallery by Richard J. Fisher.

Page 101: petroglyph dinnerware from The Chile Shop; cushion from Santa Fe Interiors.

Page 103: bowls from Santa Fe Pottery; table by Richard Comstock; carpet from Santa Fe Interiors.

Page 105: bowls from La Mesa of Santa Fe; silver cutlery from James Reid, Ltd.; wood table from African Odyssey.

Page 107: antique Native American basket from Joshua Baer; background painting by Eduardo Fuss.

Page 111: wooden bowl from African Odyssey.

Page 113: glass bowl by Melissa Haid; spoon from Casa Ana.

Page 115: plate from Nambé; spoon from Cookworks.

Page 117: the background painting is *Invitados Penosos* (detail), oil on canvas, by Leovigildo Martinez.

Page 119: silver service from Casa Ana; Spanish shawl from Nathalie.

Page 121: plate by Christy Teetor.

Page 123: glasses from Tesuque Glass Works by Michael Hatch.

Shops & Artists

African Odyssey create their tables and other furniture from hardwood railroad ties laid in South Africa at the turn of the century. Sena Plaza, 126 East Palace, Santa Fe, NM 87501. Tel: (505) 820-7377.

Casa Ana has an extensive collection of the finest Spanish Colonial, Old English, Arts and Crafts, Art Deco and Aesthetic Period silverware. It also carries beautiful pieces for the novice collector. 503 Canyon Road, Santa Fe, NM 87501. Tel: (505) 989-1781.

Marie Romero Cash, a native of Santa Fe, is an accomplished artist whose work can be found in the Smithsonian Institution as well as other museums and private collections. The primitive-looking *santos* that are her specialty were first carved by early settlers of the Southwest to make up for the lack of religious art in early New Mexican churches. *Santos* have traditionally been carved by male *santeros,* but Marie Romero Cash is one of the growing number of *santeras* who are gaining recognition for their work.

The Chile Shop sells traditional and contemporary houseware from Santa Fe. Dishes, linens, *ristras* and ingredients are all available through their mail order catalog. 109 East Water Street, Santa Fe, NM 87501. Tel: (505) 983-6080.

Richard Comstock specializes in sculpting stone and iron tables and garden furniture. He can be found at **Trader Jack's Flea Market**.

Cookworks stocks a wide variety of items in three general areas—professional kitchen equipment, tabletop items, particularly imported Italian and French dinnerware, and gourmet food items. They also have an extensive line of cookbooks. 322 South Guadalupe Street, Santa Fe, NM 87501. Tel: (800) 972-3357.

Cutlery of Santa Fe has been in business for over twenty years specializing in fine kitchen utensils and serving pieces, especially inlaid wood.107 Old Santa Fe Trail, La Fonda Hotel, Santa Fe, NM 87501. Tel: (505) 982-3262.

Megin Diamond's beautiful silver pieces can be found at **Casa Ana**.

Richard J. Fisher is an accomplished and versatile tinsmith and artist who has been working with tin, brass and copper for over ten years. His works are original hand-stamped northern New Mexico tinwork. He can be found at his studio and gallery, Tinwork Studio and Gallery, in Tesuque, New Mexico. Tel: (505) 989-4227.

Merry Elizabeth Foss is a dealer of older Peruvian and Bolivian collectibles, including textiles, silver, jewelry, religious and folk pieces and oddities. She can be found at **Trader Jack's Flea Market** or contacted at: 900 Los Lovatos, Santa Fe, NM 87501. Tel: (505) 982-9776.

Galeria el Zocalo, Cafe Pasqual's gallery, exhibits the work of **Leovigildo Martinez** and is his sole representative in North America. 54½ East San Francisco, Santa Fe, NM 87501. Tel: (505) 984-2901.

Galería Hispánica sells fine crafts, among them the ceramic dishware of the Aguilar family. Augustín Aguilar is the first modern Talavera potter, as well as the first modern artist to be accepted by the Museum of International Folk Art in Santa Fe. Each lead-free, durable piece is made by hand at the family's shop in Mexico. Galería Hispánica is in La Fonda Hotel, 100 East San Francisco, Santa Fe, NM 87501. Tel: (505) 982-4549.

Gift n Gourmet sells unique dinnerware by local craftspeople, glassware, cookware, gadgets, linens, tiles and knives. 55 Old Santa Fe Trail, Santa Fe, NM 87501. Tel: (800) 656-3234.

Glen Green Galleries has an eclectic selection of works by contemporary American and international artists with locations in Santa Fe and Scottsdale, Arizona. Their Santa Fe shop is at 50 East San Francisco Street, Santa Fe, NM 87501. Tel: (505) 988-4168.

Griffith Ranch Trading Company features one-of-a-kind treasures such as hand carved dolls, jewelry, leather throws and pillows, fine art and folk art created by a select group of New Mexican artists and craftspeople. **Daryl Griffith** works on the premises painting furniture, bird houses, boot jacks and wooden books. 924 Paseo de Peralta, Number 2, Santa Fe, NM 87501. Phone and fax: (505) 995-0119.

Melissa Haid has been creating her plates and dishes by carefully sandwiching beads between layers of window glass for the past ten years. Her goal is to create artwork that can turn ordinary events, such as eating, into celebrations. She can be found at **Trader Jack's Flea Market**.

Michael Hatch is an artist and hot shop technician at **Tesuque Glass Works**. He has been in a variety of shows and exhibitions around the United States.

James Holmes is a formally trained sculptor who lives in Santa Fe. He fabricates his pieces from wood, as well as more unusual media—a vinyl record that has been heated in a microwave and buffalo horns are two examples. He can be found at **Trader Jack's Flea Market** or contacted at (505) 474-5218.

In Home Furnishings sells antique furnishings and accessories from Spain and Italy. The store has been in business for eight years and is located at 132 East Marcy Street, Santa Fe, NM 87501. Tel: (505) 983-0808.

James Reid, Ltd. sells tip sets, belts, jewelry, artwork, furniture and cutlery. 114 East Palace Avenue, Santa Fe, NM 87501. Tel: (505) 988-1147.

Joshua Baer & Company carries classic American Indian art, especially collections of Navajo, Pueblo, and Rio Grande wearing blankets and baskets. 116 ½ East Palace Avenue, Santa Fe, NM 87501. Tel: (505) 988-8944.

Kelly Jo Kuchar designs beautiful, handmade, functional tabletop artwork that is sold through her store, **Kelly Jo Designs**. Each unique piece is lead-free, non-toxic, and microwave and dishwasher safe. She can be found at **Trader Jack's Flea Market** or

421 Morningside Drive, SE, Albuquerque, NM 87108. Tel: (800) 844-5060.

La Mesa of Santa Fe features the finest hand-crafted platters, glassware, linens, furniture, pottery, fine art and accessories, particularly contemporary designs by New Mexican artisans. 225 Canyon Road, Santa Fe, NM 87501. Tel: (505) 984-1688.

Heidi Loewen is a porcelain artist who works primarily with wheel thrown forms. She creates swirled and colored porcelains influenced by sources as diverse as Asian design and the New Mexican skies and mountains. Heidi is the founding director of Santa Fe Artworks, a school for sculpture and clay pieces. Her pieces are in collections around the world. Tel: (505) 988-2225.

Gregory Lomayesva combines pop art and traditional Hopi images in his figures, masks and paintings. He is the son of Bill Lomayesva, a carver and jewelry designer, and **Marie Romero Cash**. His work is in several collections around the world and can be found at **La Mesa of Santa Fe**.

Davis and Christine Mather have been dealing in New Mexican animal wood carvings, Native American and Hispanic arts since 1976. Christine Mather is an art historian and was curator of the Spanish Colonial collection at the Museum of International Folk Art. **Davis Mather Folk Art Gallery**, 141 Lincoln Avenue, Santa Fe, NM 87501. Tel: (505) 983-1660.

Rosalea Murphy, the owner and chef of The Pink Adobe, is a pioneer of the restaurant business in Santa Fe and a talented painter.

Leovigildo Martinez, a native of Oaxaca, Mexico, paints these vibrant oil pieces, several of which enliven the walls of Cafe Pasqual's. The **Galeria el Zocalo** is his representative in North America.

Nambé has been creating unique sand-cast tableware, home accessories and gifts in the Sangre de Cristo Mountains since 1951. Their pieces, which are made of a special alloy that does not contain silver, lead or pewter, are created by dedicated craftsmen and artisans. 1127 Siler Road, Santa Fe, NM 87505. Tel: (505) 471-2912.

Nathalie is a source for fine Western and European clothing and home furnishings. During the summer months, artisans demonstrate their crafts in the store's courtyard. 503 Canyon Road, Santa Fe, NM 87501. Tel: (505) 982-1021.

Fredrick Prescot's steel sculptures can be seen at Houshangs Gallery at 713 Canyon Road in Santa Fe.

Rainbow Gate is a small dinnerware company founded in the fall of 1994 by Allan Walter and Jenny Lind. Each piece is handmade and painted with layers of different colors to achieve rich hues and patterns. 530 South Guadalupe Street, Santa Fe, NM 87501. Tel: (505) 983-8892.

Emilio Romero, Jr., a sculptor, was born in Santa Fe. He creates hand-wrought copper objects, but also works in other metals. His work has been exhibited at El Fino Gallery in Taos.

Santa Fe Interiors specializes in one hundred percent wool Zapotec Indian rugs; they also do custom orders and contemporary designs. 214 Old Santa Fe Trail, Santa Fe, NM 87501. Tel: (505) 988-2227.

Santa Fe Pottery represents the work of master potters from New Mexico and the Southwest. The store features dinnerware, baking and serving pieces, lighting fixtures as well as many gift items. 323 South Guadalupe Street, Santa Fe, NM 87501. Tel: (505) 989-3363

Santa Fe School of Cooking and Market features a full selection of Southwest cookbooks, as well as hard-to-find ingredients and food products to capture the taste, look and scent of Santa Fe. Upper Level, Plaza Mercado, 116 West San Francisco Street, Santa Fe, NM 87501. Tel: (505) 983-4511, fax: (505) 983-7540, orders: (800) 982-4688.

Seckler Studio Frank H. Seckler and his son Frank

B. Seckler have been designing and executing hand-fabricated steel pieces for eleven years and have stores in Taos, Santa Fe and Denver. In addition to the pieces in their studios, the two also do custom work. 150 South St. Francis Drive, Santa Fe, NM 87501.Tel: (505) 989-4370.

Christy Teetor, based in Albuquerque, was a painter before she studied pottery and has brought a painter's eye to the creation of her ceramic ornaments, platters and dishes. Christy's work is inspired by the colors of the Sandia and Manzo Mountains. She can be found at **Trader Jack's Flea Market** or contacted at P.O. Box 10172, Albuquerque, NM 87184. Tel: (505) 897-6479.

Tesuque Glass Works was founded in 1975 by Charlie Miner. The glass shop gives people the opportunity to watch the steps of glass blowing in the beautiful setting of Tesuque. P.O. Box 146, Bishops Lodge Road, Tesuque, NM 87574. Tel: (505) 988-2165.

Trader Jack's Flea Market, known unofficially as the Santa Fe Flea Market, is a gathering spot for many of the artists whose works are in this book, as well as many other exciting local artists. The market is open weekends from March through November off highway 84/285 in Tesuque.

Trompe Deluxe was started by Karen Browne and Elaine Roy two years ago to create hand painted canvas floorcloths, cushions and tapestries. 1218 Tijeras Street, N.E., Albuquerque, NM 87106. Tel: (505) 766-5415.

Acknowledgments

The publisher would like to thank Robert Shure, Marie Romero Cash, Peggy Jackson, Robin Ann Powell, Rosalea Murphy, Christy Teetor, Emilio Romero, Jr., Gregory Lomayesva and Heidi Loewen for their generosity and their willingness to open their homes and studios to us; Jose L. Villegas, Sr. at the State Records Center and Archives and the staff at the Palace of Governors; and Denice Skrepcinski for her invaluable help in preparing the food for photography. A very special thank you to Paula Summers who helped in innumerable ways and to Mrs Ong for her culinary expertise and eye for detail, and to the many chefs and artists for their enthusiastic participation in this project. And to the people of Santa Fe, a big thank you for their warmth and hospitality.

Index

Boldface type indicates the page on which a photograph appears.